Artful Paper Dolls

NEW WAYS TO PLAY

WITH A TRADITIONAL FORM

Artful Paper Dolls

NEW WAYS TO PLAY

WITH A TRADITIONAL FORM

TERRY TAYLOR

LARK BOOKS

A Division of Sterling Publishing Co., Inc.

New York / London

ART DIRECTOR
Susan McBride

COVER DESIGNER
Barbara Zaretsky

ASSOCIATE EDITOR
Nathalie Mornu

ASSOCIATE ART DIRECTOR
Shannon Yokeley

ART PRODUCTION
Jeff Hamilton

EDITORIAL ASSISTANCE
Dawn Dillingham
Delores Gosnell

EDITORIAL INTERNS
David Squires
Sue Stigleman

ART INTERNS
Ardyce E. Alspach
Emily Kepley
Nathan Schulman

PHOTOGRAPHER
Steve Mann

Cover photo by
Doug Van De Zande.
Photo on page 86 by
Doug Van De Zande.

The Library of Congress has cataloged the hardcover edition as follows:

Taylor, Terry, 1952-
 Artful paper dolls : new ways to play with a traditional form /
Terry Taylor.
   p. cm.
 Includes index.
 ISBN 1-57990-715-6 (hardcover)
 1. Paper dolls. 2. Altered books. I. Title.
TT175.T39 2006
745.592'21--dc22

                              2005032364

10 9 8 7 6 5 4 3 2

Published by Lark Books, A Division of
Sterling Publishing Co., Inc.
387 Park Avenue South, New York, N.Y. 10016

First Paperback Edition 2009
Text © 2006, Lark Books
Photography © 2006, Lark Books unless otherwise specified
Illustrations © 2006, Lark Books unless otherwise specified

Distributed in Canada by Sterling Publishing,
c/o Canadian Manda Group, 165 Dufferin Street
Toronto, Ontario, Canada M6K 3H6

Distributed in the United Kingdom by GMC Distribution Services,
Castle Place, 166 High Street, Lewes, East Sussex, England BN7 1XU

Distributed in Australia by Capricorn Link (Australia) Pty Ltd.,
P.O. Box 704, Windsor, NSW 2756 Australia

If you have questions or comments about this book, please contact:
Lark Books
67 Broadway
Asheville, NC 28801
(828) 253-0467

Manufactured in China

ISBN 13: 978-1-57990-715-0 (hardcover) 978-1-60059-480-9 (paperback)

For information about custom editions, special sales, premium and
corporate purchases, please contact Sterling Special Sales Department
at 800-805-5489 or specialsales@sterlingpub.com.

CONTENTS

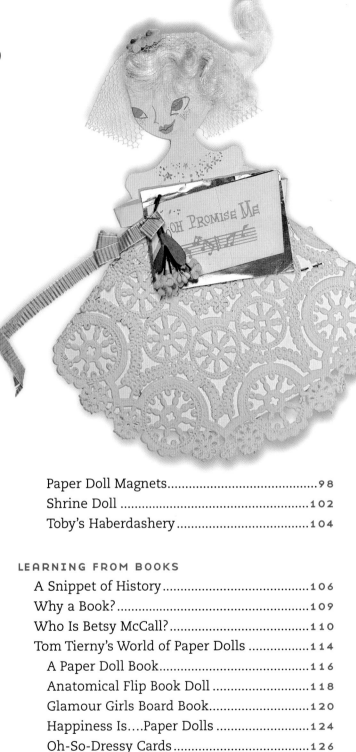

INTRODUCTION

I'VE GOT A SECRET TO TELL YOU:
I've always loved paper dolls.

My maternal cousins are girls (well, they're grown women now). When I started working on this book, I asked my aunt to ask my cousin, Lucy, if she remembered playing paper dolls with me. Lucy vaguely remembered playing with paper dolls with me. She told her mother that if she had wanted to play with paper dolls, she probably would have tried talking me into playing with her. Truth be told, she never had to twist my arm to get me to play with paper dolls. In fact, I may have begged Lucy to play with paper dolls with me.

If you're reading this introduction, my guess is that you love paper dolls as much as I do. How long has it been since you've even thought about them? After all, busy adults with grown-up lives don't play with paper dolls. But there's no reason why we shouldn't. We knit, create paper crafts, make dolls, or dabble with altered art. The paper doll is simply another creative canvas to explore. It can be a plaything, the starting point for journaling meaningful experiences, or an artistic expression.

Do you remember being trapped indoors on rainy afternoons? Mothers with foresight prepared for just such an event with an uncut book of paper dolls ready to pull out of their bag of tricks. Or perhaps they would give us simple tools and materials—pencil, paper, crayons, and blunt-nosed scissors—and help us create our own paper dolls. You'll use the same simple tools and materials to create unique paper dolls today—but now you can use sharp, pointed scissors.

For many of us, paper dolls have held a special place in our lives. We saw paper doll imagery in advertising, heard popular songs about paper dolls, and dressed our favorite film and television stars. I, for one, pored longingly over my grandmother's back issues of *McCall's*—she didn't allow us to cut out Betsy McCall (see page 104).

I've had plenty of experience making paper dolls. In 2nd grade I learned to make origami dolls. Two years later I specialized in drawing a stylized geisha figure over and over again. (I think I could still draw that same figure

vintage images to revive childhood memories. You'll also see the work of many talented artists to inspire you in both the gallery images and in the projects.

I hope you'll have as much fun playing with paper dolls as I did making and writing about them. You don't need it, but you have my permission to play with paper dolls again and forever more. If you've never played with paper dolls, prepare to fall in love with them. Now, grab your scissors, throw caution to the wind, and run with them straight to your worktable.

in exactly the same way now.) At some point, I realized I should just draw one geisha, and make dozens of elaborately patterned kimonos for it. (Even then, I knew about tabs.) While others were spending their allowances on action comic books, I preferred *Katy Keene* (see page 62).

It didn't stop there. In the early 1960s I was completely enthralled with all things mod and Carnaby Street. I drew figures featuring Twiggy's outsized eyelashes and shockingly short bob. And let me point out here that I was not very good at drawing, but it didn't matter. I was more interested in creating a paper wardrobe for the figure. Then, I figured out that I could make dolls and dresses using colorful magazine pictures: I didn't have to draw at all!

I had a really good time making just a few projects for this book. I wouldn't have minded making even more if I hadn't found so many talented and generous people to play paper dolls with me. Shopping online for most of the vintage paper dolls and ephemera you'll see in this book was even more fun.

I've divided this book into four chapters, each based on a different aspect of creating paper dolls: the figure, the dress, the house, and the book form. In each chapter you'll find a snippet of paper doll history with plenty of

The Paper Doll song written in 1915 by John Stewart Black became a hit song for the vocal group the Mills Brothers in 1943. It spent 12 weeks on the charts and sold over 6 million copies, including sheet music. *Edward B. Marks Music Corporation, New York, New York, 1943*

FIGURING IT OUT

A Snippet of History

In this age of virtual information and electronic toys it's easy to forget that dolls—representations of the human figure—weren't always thought of as play things. In the not-too-distant past, people took dolls seriously, and dolls served different purposes in cultures around the world. They were (and still are) used as charms, talismans, and fetishes—not for children to play with, but for a medicine man or sorcerer to handle.

In ancient Japan, fishermen placed dolls on their boats for protection. If a storm developed, they threw the dolls into the water as substitutes for the lives on board. In Mexico, a *bruja* or *brujo* of the Otomi Indian tribe cut

Drunken Man with Large Hat, a Japanese folded paper doll.
PHOTO © BLAIR CLARK. MUSEUM OF INTERNATIONAL FOLK ART. SANTA FE, NEW MEXICO. DEPT. OF CULTURAL AFFAIRS

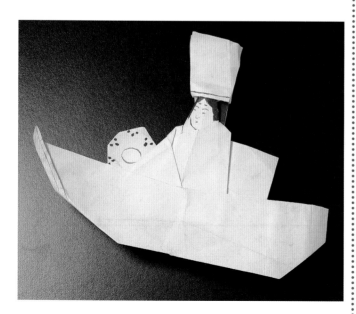

Woman Riding in Boat, is a Japanese folded paper doll
PHOTO © BLAIR CLARK. MUSEUM OF INTERNATIONAL FOLK ART. SANTA FE, NEW MEXICO. DEPT. OF CULTURAL AFFAIRS

out paper dolls from bark paper (*amate*). The dolls were embellished with vegetative motifs such as corn or beans, and then buried in the fields to ensure a good crop.

Through the centuries, people began to use dolls more for educational purposes and playthings, rather than ritual objects. *Hina Matsuri*, or Girl's Day Festival, is celebrated in Japan on the third day of the third month. This holiday evolved out of ancient purification rituals involving the use of special folded paper dolls that were rubbed on the skin to purify the soul; the sins of the soul were then sent sailing on a river or up in smoke.

An Otomi cutout figure made of light and natural amate paper from San Pablito, Puebla, Mexico

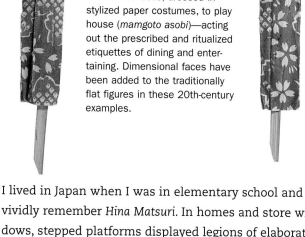

Japanese *anesama ningyos* (elder sister dolls) first appeared during the 16th century. Originally court ladies made them for adult amusement. Later, young girls used these dolls, dressed in stylized paper costumes, to play house (*mamgoto asobi*)—acting out the prescribed and ritualized etiquettes of dining and entertaining. Dimensional faces have been added to the traditionally flat figures in these 20th-century examples.

I lived in Japan when I was in elementary school and vividly remember *Hina Matsuri*. In homes and store windows, stepped platforms displayed legions of elaborately dressed and coifed dolls representing the emperor's court. At the top sat the emperor and empress dolls, their many courtiers arrayed in order of status below them. These dolls weren't for play; they were regarded as objects of beauty, and every young girl desired at least a small set of them. In our American grade school, we were exposed to Japanese culture in a class that, to my second-grade tastes, we didn't get to attend nearly often enough. During *Hina Matsuri* we folded simple origami forms representing the emperor and empress dolls. I happily made ranks and ranks of them on my own, adding color and simple designs to the folded figures.

In western cultures, paper dolls began to appear as advances in printing processes and the availability of factory-made paper gave rise to widespread production of books, newspapers, and magazines for all levels of society. Magazines such as *Godey's Lady's Book* (1830–1898) featured illustrations of the newest fashions with drawings of figures in the latest gowns. Printed drawings supplanted the elegant doll-size mannequins used to spread fashion trends.

As manufactured paper became less expensive and widely available, companies used it to create toys for children. Mass-produced paper toys were within the reach of anyone with a few pennies to spare. The first paper dolls manufactured as playthings were created in London in 1810. They were soon exported to other countries in Europe and the United States.

Even in the early 1800s, dolls made in the likeness of individual celebrities were popular. One of the first celebrity paper dolls was Marie Taglioni. If you're an admirer of the work of Joseph Cornell, you may recognize her name. One of his more famous works—*Taglioni's Jewel Casket* (1940)—is his homage to this famous ballerina. Cornell haunted vintage book and antique shops, gathering ephemera and source material for his creations. I rather like to imagine that the great man might have even purchased a Taglioni paper doll with the intention of using it in one of his works.

Creative young girls in the early 20th century may have used advertising art such as this to create their paper doll figures. *Pictorial Review, July, 1934, Pictorial Review Company, New York, New York*

Creating a Figure

The human figure is the underlying structure for all paper dolls. It can be any size, from miniscule to life-sized. Realistically drawn, given lifelike fiber hair and outfitted in fabric clothes, or rendered abstractly and composed of geometric forms and shapes, the figure is instantly recognizable. The viewer reads the shape as a human figure. But as you'll see, the paper doll form isn't limited to only the Homo sapiens species.

Many of us fondly remember the store-bought paper dolls we played with. I for one, fondly remember a cardboard doll with real blonde hair that mysteriously disappeared when we moved overseas. Even more, we may remember the paper dolls we drew for ourselves. And if we're lucky, someone has lovingly tucked them away over the years. Making paper dolls is often one of the first art and craft ventures that girls (and sometimes, boys) tackle after they've developed drawing skills and learned to use scissors.

Miriam Zaretsky lovingly saved these tiny—little more than 2½ inches (6.4 cm) tall—paper dolls. They were hand-drawn, colored, and cut out (with her help) by her young daughters Barbara and Harlene, in the 1960s.

Gwendolyn McLarty, *Postcard*, 2005
Copper, enamel, assembled images, mica, stamp, 5½ x 3½ x ¼ in. (14 x 9 x .8 cm) PHOTO © JACK ZILKER

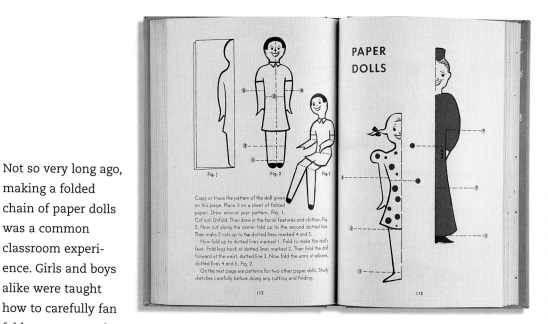

Inside the illustration:

PAPER DOLLS

Fig. 1   Fig. 2   Fig. 3

Copy or trace the pattern of the doll given on this page. Place it on a sheet of folded paper. Draw around your pattern. Fig. 1.
Cut out. Unfold. Then draw in the facial features and clothes. Fig. 2. Now cut along the center fold up to the second dotted line. Then make 2 cuts up to the dotted lines marked 4 and 5.
Now fold up to dotted lines marked 1. Fold to make the doll's feet. Fold legs back at dotted lines marked 2. Then fold the doll forward at the waist, dotted line 3. Now fold the arms at elbows, dotted lines 4 and 5. Fig. 2.
On the next page are patterns for two other paper dolls. Study sketches carefully before doing any cutting and folding.

112   113

If you're worried about making a figure symmetrical, simply fold a sheet of paper in half and sketch half of a figure on it. *Things to Make and Do, Standard Education Society, 1952*

Not so very long ago, making a folded chain of paper dolls was a common classroom experience. Girls and boys alike were taught how to carefully fan fold one or several joined-together sheets of paper. We drew a rudimentary body shape on the top folded sheet and cut out the shape with blunt-nosed scissors. No one worried about drawing the figure accurately (we were children, after all), and you shouldn't either, as you begin to make figures for paper dolls.

There aren't any hard-and-fast rules for creating a figure, but there are lots of figure styles to choose from and more ways to make them than you can shake a stick at—so to speak. The simplest way to make a figure is to draw a simple outline of a human figure—such as a gingerbread man shape—just as you did when you made paper doll chains.

If you never made a paper doll chain, I suggest—no, I *insist*—that you stop right here. Gather several sheets of paper and grab some scissors (but don't run with them). Glue or tape the sheets together, fan-fold them, and draw a figure on the top fold with one hand and one foot touching the fold. Cut out the figure (be sure you don't cut the fold) and unfold the chain. Pretty easy, isn't it? A kindergarten student can do that. Now, allow your creative adult self to play by drawing, coloring, or collaging the forms. After you finish, turn to page 88 and see how one grown-up artist adapts that simple paper doll chain form.

The standard for a human figure consists of two arms, two legs, a torso, and a head. Let's face it: we're not all artists who draw both accurately and realistically. Should you need some help with the proportions of your figure, remember the seven-and-a-half head rule that artists have used through the centuries. It approximates the natural proportion of the body. Fashion illustrators deliberately stretch their figures to eight or nine heads in height for an exaggerated effect. Both are instantly recognizable as human. However, there's something inherently charming (or perhaps creepily disturbing) about figures with oddly proportioned body parts, or even multiple limbs. Consider the effect you wish to achieve with your figure.

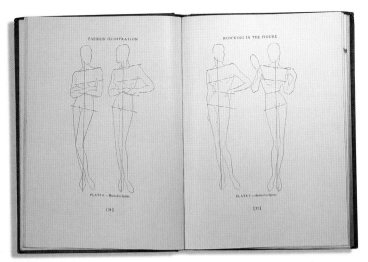

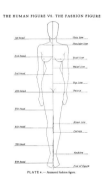

The head is the most convenient unit for measuring a figure's overall height. Determine the size of the head first; draw a faint line for each head measurement, and then draw the figure within the defined limit. Fashion figures are generally 8 to 10 heads tall to allow the illustrator to focus on the outfit. *Fashion Illustration, Christine Schmuck and Virginia Jewel, Whittlesey House, McGraw-Hill Book Company, Inc., New York and London, 1937*

One Piece or Many?

Do you want your figure to be static (in one piece) or jointed for movement? French *pantins* (also known as jumping jacks in England, and *Hamplemann* in Germany) are the archetypal jointed paper dolls. It's likely that the paper dolls that you played with as a child were one piece; very few commercially-made paper dolls featured movement.

If you want a static figure but don't care to draw your own, there are many ways to accomplish the task. For a very generic figure, trace around a gingerbread cookie cutter. If you want a more realistic figure, choose a finished figure that appeals to you (a photograph or a drawing), place tracing paper on top of it, and outline the shape.

You can also use the templates that we've provided on page 140. Though these templates were designed to create jointed figures, you can use them to make a static figure. Simply trace the template pieces, overlapping and positioning the limbs as you desire, then cut out the figure in one piece.

Another option is to cut out figures from magazines, books, or catalogs; use them wholly or as collage elements. Or, purchase vintage (or new) paper dolls and alter them as you wish. Several artists featured in this book created figures with vintage dolls (page 40), or templates of doll shapes salvaged from commercially-printed paper dolls (page 37).

You can make pantins, or jointed figures, using static figures, simply with a little judicious cutting and fastening (page 32). You'll need multiple copies of your figure to cut out and reassemble. Or, you can simply copy the templates on page 140. (We've given you a distinctly feminine figure and a large-bodied, more androgynous figure.) Use paper fasteners, eyelets, or stitching to join the pieces.

At one point in history, *pantins* were so popular and widespread that the French royal court placed a ban on them for fear they would frighten pregnant women. This contemporary example is by Dee Segula. *Courtesy of Susie Van der Vorst*

Use any method you wish to bring your paper doll to life. If you aren't satisfied with your drawing skills, don't fret about it. Human features can be abstracted, just like those emoticons you use in your emails: two dots and a curved line are all that it takes to suggest a smiling or frowning face. If you crave realism, use rubber stamps, clip art, photographs, or collage materials to create the facial expressions you desire.

In this chapter you'll discover a variety of ways that different artists have used to create their figures. I, for one, don't like the way I draw, so I created figures using disparate elements (page 22) and clip art (page 30). You'll also find paper dolls that are created digitally and printed out (pages 20 and 68) before they are cut out and assembled. One paper doll (page 28) has startled more than one person I know, and it isn't even scary! Go figure.

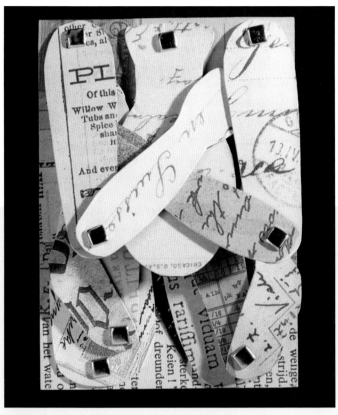

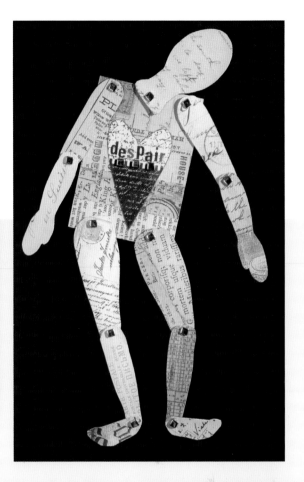

Heather Crossley, *Heart of Despair (ATC/Paper Doll)*, 2005
Paper, brads, rubber stamp, alphabet stickers, 10¾ x 10¼ in.
(27.5 x 26.5 cm) PHOTO © RUSSELL STOKES

Jane Maxwell,
Puzzled, 2003
Collage and wax
on wood blocks,
12 x 18 x 2 in.
(30.5 x 45.7
x 5.1 cm)
PHOTO © ARTIST

PAPER DOLL
PUBLISHING

Mary Gray paper doll manufactured by McLoughlin Brother, date unknown. FROM THE COLLECTIONS OF THE HENRY FORD MUSEUM (41.214.1474.2/G7069)

In 1828, John McLoughlin set up a small printing shop in New York City. By 1857, his brother Edmund had joined him, and under the name McLoughlin Brothers, they started printing paper dolls. McLoughlin Brothers was the first mass publisher of paper dolls in America, forging ahead with innovations such as tabbed clothing. Unaware of the mass appeal their paper dolls would later have, the envelopes the dolls came in identified them as mere "amusement for little girls."

Around the same time the McLoughlin brothers were getting started in the paper doll business, German-born Raphael Tuck moved to England. He opened a frame shop in London in 1886, and by 1870, his sons had helped him turn it into a full-scale publishing business. While Raphael Tuck and Sons produced all sorts of paper items, including cards, puzzles, and novelty books, their paper dolls are of particular importance. They were the first company to use heavier, more substantial cardboard to make a higher quality and longer lasting doll.

Paper dolls soon became a popular publishing item. Between the 1920s and 1960s several publishers produced dolls of movie stars as well as fictional characters. Saalfield Publishing Company of Akron, Ohio, started with Little Mary Mix-up in 1922, illustrated by R. M. Brinkerhoff. They went on to publish the immensely popular Shirley Temple paper dolls throughout the 1930s and 1940s. Saalfield continued printing paper dolls through the 1960s and was the world's largest publisher of children's materials for a while. The company went out of business in 1977, but their original Shirley Temple designs are still reprinted today.

For Saalfield to become the leading force in children's publishing, it had to compete with its notable contemporaries Western Publishing, Samuel Lowe Publishing Company, and Whitman Publishing Companies. Those three paper doll giants were all directly related to each other. In 1907, E. H. Wadewitz bought a failing printing company in Wisconsin

This large paper doll's lush costuming is a fine example of lithographic printing. *Artistic Series 501, Raphael Tuck & Sons Co, LTD, London, Paris, & New York, 1894. Courtesy of Magnolia Beauregard's, Asheville, North Carolina*

company, Samuel Lowe Publishing. By the time the company closed in 1979, the popularity of Lowe paper dolls was on par with Saalfield, Whitman, and their earlier paper doll counterparts. Half a century after the peak of paper doll popularity, fans continue to buy new and old sets to play with and collect. Companies such as Dover Publishing and B. Shackman & Co, Inc., still publish and republish the public's favorite paper dolls.

This doll has a glossy, plasticized finish. The clothing is printed on paper that has a glossy finish on both sides. It took me a few minutes to figure out how the clothes stayed on—static electricity! *Magic Stay-On Doll (No. 4618), 1963, Whitman Publishing Co., Racine, Wisconsin*

and turned it into a respected and profitable business. He renamed the company Western Printing, and sought opportunities for growth. A foreman's clerical error had left the company with an overage of hundreds of children's books, unpaid for, and the opportunity Wadewitz needed. By selling the extra books directly to retail stores, Western recuperated company losses and actually made a profit. Shortly after that, Wadewitz created the Whitman division specifically to develop children's products for the retail chain market.

With connections to retail chain stores, the Whitman division opened production to other publishable goods in the early 1920s. Their new products included jigsaw puzzles, board games, and, of course, paper dolls. Sam Lowe, president of the Whitman division, had enormous success marketing children's items, including an entire line of Disney-themed paper dolls. In 1940, however, Lowe left Western to found his own

3 RED GIRLS AND A BLONDE

Create your own personal variation of this collage using your choice of vintage paper doll imagery and Jane's techniques.

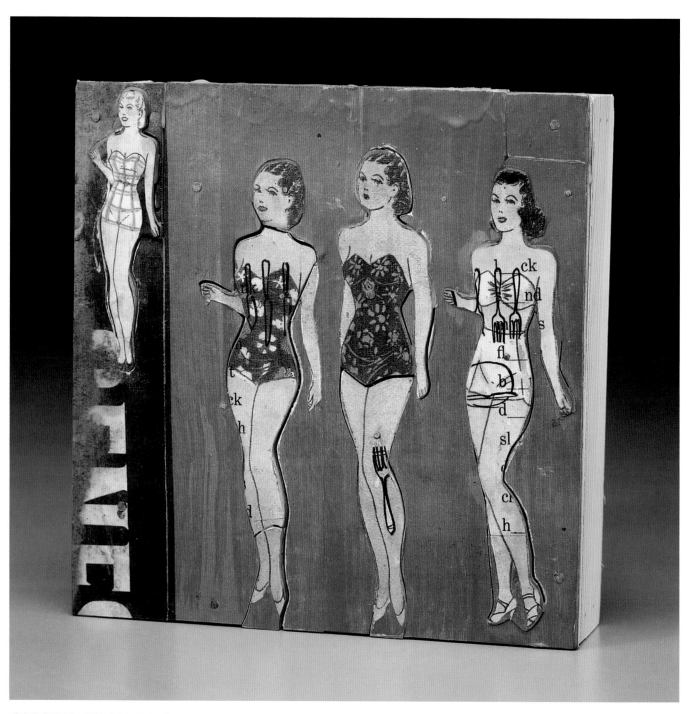

CREATED BY JANE MAXWELL

MATERIALS

Wood strips

¼-inch (6mm) plywood

Paper dolls

Decorative papers

Acrylic paint

Nails

Beeswax

1 You can build your own wood box stretcher, or purchase one from a craft or framing shop. Jane measured and cut two pieces of plywood to fit the stretcher's dimensions. One of the two pieces was attached directly to the stretcher frame.

2 Jane painted the second piece of plywood with acrylic paint, then composed a collage of vintage doll cutouts on the plywood. She added found papers and superimposed imagery of forks and knives on top of the paper doll figures.

3 She used a band saw to cut out the dolls—in jigsaw puzzle fashion—then nailed the pieces onto the plywood-covered stretcher.

4 A finish of melted beeswax was brushed onto the finished piece.

❝ *As a frequent visitor to antique markets,* *I'm always on the hunt for paper doll cutouts. Not because I played with them as a child; I didn't. And not because I especially want my daughters to play with them now; I don't. It's more as a curiosity. I want to see if I can find doll cutouts without the perfect hourglass figure and form fitting clothes. In my experience there aren't any to be found.*

Here, I used the doll cutout icon to explore the message that being thin and perfectly dressed is the desired norm and a societal expectation of young women. In this piece, the line of doll figures is meant to underscore the role that female competition plays in the ideal body quest. The physical cuts in the silhouettes symbolize women's fixation on their flawed body parts. The small, thin blonde in the upper corner represents the elusive, idealized goal. ❞
Jane Maxwell

COG9TIVE ROBOT

Stretch your creative muscles and gather up a wide assortment of gadgets and hardware. Then mull over the possibilities they have for arms, legs, and (perhaps) two or more heads.

CREATED BY SHANNON YOKELEY

MATERIALS

Computer
Digital camera
Computer parts
Hardware
Clip art
Poster board
Spray adhesive
Paper fasteners
Metal scrapbook
embellishments

1 Shannon gathered actual computer parts, assorted hardware, and sheets of metal. She either photographed them with her digital camera or scanned them with her computer.

2 Shannon used a photo manipulation program to size the images and to add or change their color.

3 She imported the imagery into a layout or desktop publishing program. Then she used the program to piece together the parts of the robot before she printed them out.

4 Shannon printed out the pieces using a color printer. She mounted them onto poster board with a spray adhesive before she cut them out.

5 Once the parts were cut out, Shannon used paper fasteners to join them. She added scrapbook embellishments to spell out her robot's name.

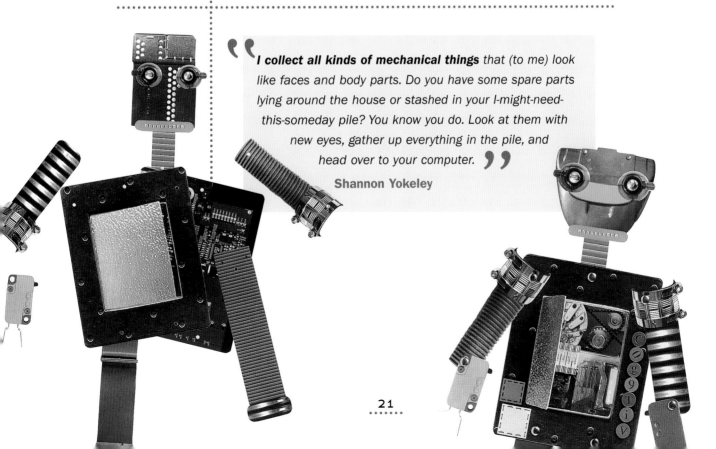

I collect all kinds of mechanical things that (to me) look like faces and body parts. Do you have some spare parts lying around the house or stashed in your I-might-need-this-someday pile? You know you do. Look at them with new eyes, gather up everything in the pile, and head over to your computer. **"**

Shannon Yokeley

DISJOINTED FIGURE

There's no reason why you have to make a single figure with multiple dresses to wear. Go ahead, break the rule: Make many figures that share the same dress.

CREATED BY TERRY TAYLOR

Postcards
Magazines
Photographs
Cardstock
Paper fasteners

1 I searched my postcard collection for costume postcards from museum collections. (I have boxes and boxes filled with postcards.) I also asked a friend who was vacationing in London to look for similar cards at the Victoria and Albert Museum. I chose one card out of all of the ones in my collection to use for this paper doll.

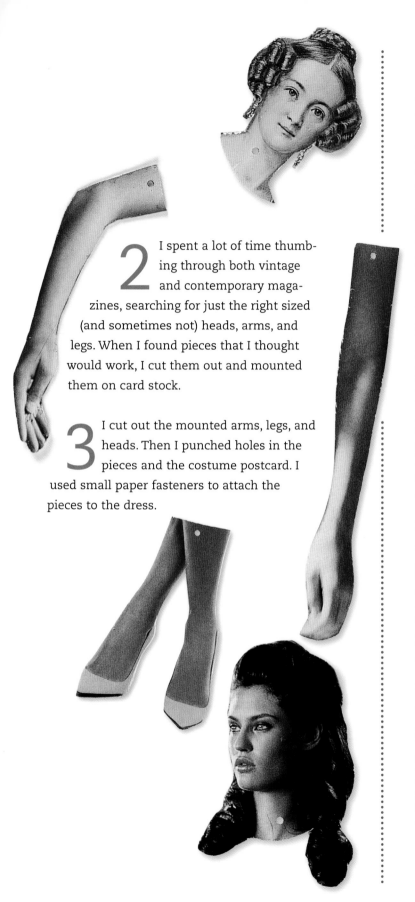

2 I spent a lot of time thumbing through both vintage and contemporary magazines, searching for just the right sized (and sometimes not) heads, arms, and legs. When I found pieces that I thought would work, I cut them out and mounted them on card stock.

3 I cut out the mounted arms, legs, and heads. Then I punched holes in the pieces and the costume postcard. I used small paper fasteners to attach the pieces to the dress.

Melissa Loen, *Natasha Paper Doll*, 2002
Paper, found imagery, 10½ x 2¾ in. (27 x 7 cm)
PHOTO © ARTIST

These two early 20th century figures have dresses cut out from one source and heads from another.

Above, **Julie A. Fremuth**, *Please See Me*, 2004
Accordion panel book with jointed figures made with paper, board, gouache, pencil, colored pencil, house paint, rivets, 7½ x 25½ x ½ in. (19 x 65 x 1 cm) closed, 7½ x 15 ¼ in. (19 x 38.5 cm) open. PHOTO © LON HORWEDEL

EAT MORE SOUP

This figure doesn't follow the seven-and-a-half head rule, but it's instantly recognizable as a human figure. You can see how the figure grows, from head to toe, with Lynn's whimsical choices for body parts.

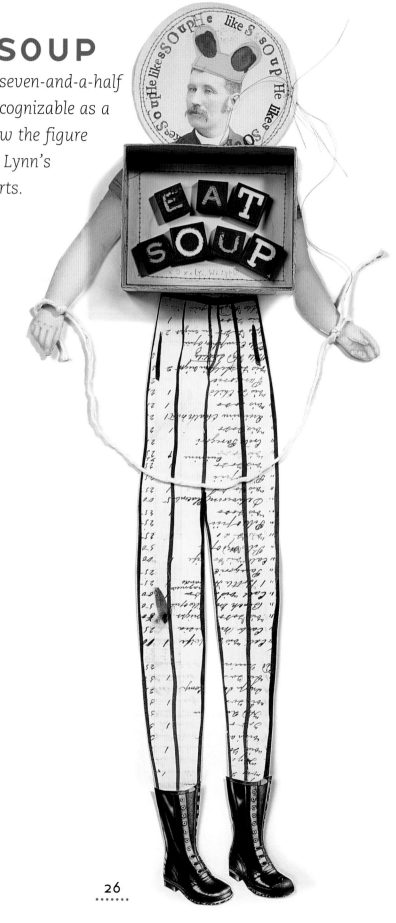

MATERIALS

Vintage photograph

Vintage paper doll

Card stock

Decorative papers

Vintage ledger paper

Vintage mail-order catalog

Box

Rubber-stamp alphabet

Marker

Game pieces

Twine

CREATED BY LYNN WHIPPLE

1 Lynn photocopied a vintage photograph in color. She stamped text around the head and created a very special hat for her gentleman. She machine stitched around the circle to add visual interest.

2 Then she selected the arm and shoulder portion of a vintage paper doll. (Was it a fragment or did she dismember the doll? You decide.) The size of the arms, in turn, more or less determined her choice for the length of the legs.

3 Lynn sketched legs on vintage ledger paper, tapering them to fit the pictures of work boots she found in a mail-order catalog. She outlined the legs with marker, cut them out, and glued the boots in place.

4 To assemble the doll, Lynn sketched a very simple body shape on card stock. She cut it out and glued the head, arms, and legs to the form.

5 Lynn embellished the box with stitched decorative paper that matched the sleeves of the shirt. She glued the game pieces inside, then glued the box in place. She embellished the finished doll with a short jump rope made of twine.

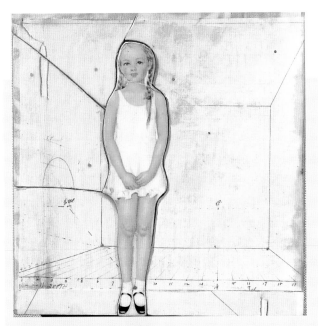

Jane Maxwell, *Doll Girl,* 2004
Collage, wood, wax, 8 x 8 x 2 in. (20.3 x 20.3 x 5.1 cm)
PHOTO © ARTIST

Nicole McConville, *Guardian,* 2004
Wooden boxes, photos, found text, optical lens, dictionary definition, paper, beeswax, rusted metal, 9½ x 12½ x 3 in. (24.1 x 31.8 x 7.6 cm) PHOTO © STEVE MANN

ELISABETH'S DOPPELGÄNGER

Elisabeth's father—an editor at Lark Books—is always unnerved when he turns the corner into the office where Elisabeth is stored. I don't find her unnerving, but then she's not my daughter. Why not make your own life-sized doll?

CREATED BY DANA IRWIN

Photograph
Computer
Foam-core board
Spray adhesive
Wallpaper samples
Buttons

1 Dana photographed her subject. There's no reason your subject has to be a child. It could just as well be your partner or your pet!

2 Dana scanned the photograph at 300 dpi and adjusted the scanned photo to the desired size. Then she loaded the image onto a disc.

3 She took the disc to a local copy shop and they printed out in color, in sections.

4 Dana took the printed sections, pieced them together, and mounted each section onto foam-core board. She used a very sharp craft knife to carefully cut out the whole figure, then used a foam sanding sponge to smooth any rough edges. She created an easel back from foam-core board to allow the doll to stand unsupported.

Dana was inspired to create her doll's dress with this uncut sheet of vintage dresses.

5 Dana scanned and enlarged a vintage paper doll dress and matching hat. She printed out the dress in sections, then pieced it together to make a base for her dress. She adjusted and pieced the dress as needed to the figure's shape. Using the dress as a template, Dana cut a finished dress out of a wallpaper sample and hand-stitched buttons to the dress. Using the same method, Dana made a matching hat.

6 Paper dolls rarely have matching shoes to go with an outfit, but Dana felt that the dress needed a matching hat and shoes. She traced around the feet to make templates for the shoes and socks, then added tabs to the shapes, cut them out, and glued decorative papers on the shoes and anklets. Buttons made perfect embellishments.

Dottie Darling's Boy Friend—
Huskie Horace, *Pictorial Review,*
July 1934

A doll named Mrs. Munroe and
some of her clothes, drawn by
the heiress Gertrude Vanderbilt
Whitney. COURTESY OF WHITNEY
MUSEUM OF AMERICAN ART,
GERTRUDE VANDERBILT WHITNEY
PAPERS [CA. 1850]-1976,
IN THE ARCHIVES OF AMERICAN ART,
SMITHSONIAN INSTITUTION,
GIFT OF FLORA MILLER IRVING.

La Calavera Catrin(a)

Even skeletons like to dress up once in a while, but perhaps they're tired of basic black. Why not indulge your sense of whimsy and dress them in bright and cheery outfits?

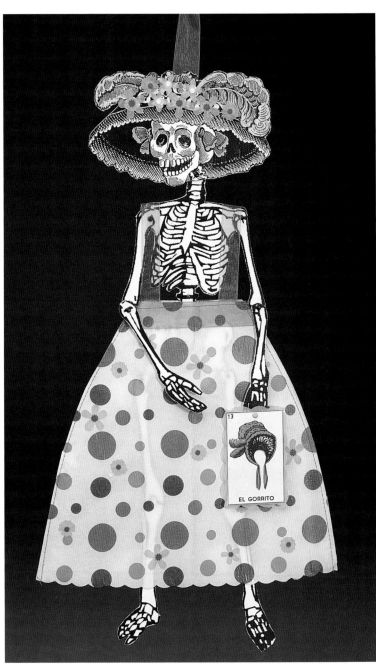

CREATED BY TERRY TAYLOR

MATERIALS

Clip art

Poster board

Colored pencils and pens

Paper fasteners

Tissue papers

Ribbon

Scrapbooking embellishments

Spray adhesive

Loteria cards

1 I found free clip art images of a skeleton and enlarged it on a photocopier. I made several copies of the skeleton in order to create the jointed pantin.

I enlarged the catrin and catrina heads, added masking fluid to parts of the images to simplify them, then recopied them, reducing them to fit the skeleton torso. The two heads share the same body.

2 Touches of color were added to both heads. I embellished the catrina's extravagant chapeaux with small vellum flower stickers.

3 I cut apart entire arms and legs. Then I cut out shoulder, rib cage, and hip sections in a single piece. I mounted the photocopies onto poster board with a spray adhesive.

"*The iconic imagery of dia de los muertos* (Day of the Dead), bold colors of Mexican folk art, and José Guadalupe Posada's popular Mexican prints inspired this double-duty pantin. And, to be honest, making a skeletal paper doll made me giggle. Is there anything better than making yourself happy while you work?"
Terry Taylor

4 To make the jointed pieces, I cut four arms and hands from the shoulders—two left and two right. I drew a small tab at the elbow of one upper arm bone, then cut out the arm bone including the tab at the elbow.

I cut out the lower arm bone and hand. Then I placed the lower arm on top of the tab, punched a small hole, and used a paper fastener to join the two parts.

This technique was used to join the upper arms to the shoulders, the legs to the hips, and either head to the neck. See why I made several photocopies?

5 I made two skirt shapes of plain paper and adhered printed tissue to the shapes with the adhesive. I stitched ribbon suspenders to one skirt, hung the ribbon over the shoulders, then matched the position of the second skirt. I taped the suspenders to the second skirt, then stitched them in place. Then I stitched the two skirts together along the side seams. There's no reason you couldn't glue the ribbon and skirt edges together if you wish.

6 I made a paper pattern for a vest to fit over the shoulders of the skeleton torso. Basically it was a large rectangle folded in half. I glued tissue to both sides, then made a cut in the center to create folded-back lapels. I added a flower-shape paper fastener to each side as a boutonnière.

7 I made a bow tie shape out of two pieces of paper and stitched it together, leaving the center unstitched in order to slip it over the neck of the skeleton.

8 *Lotería* cards or a box of wax matches were added as embellishments for each figure. Each embellishment is attached to the hand with a small paper fastener.

9 I glued a looped length of ribbon to each head as a hanging device.

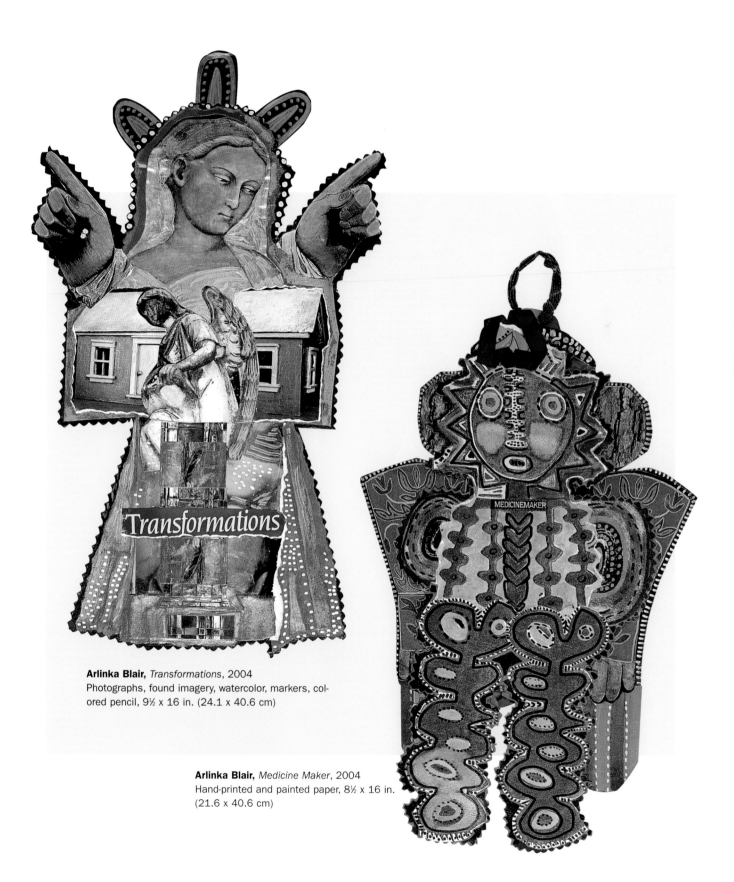

Arlinka Blair, *Transformations*, 2004
Photographs, found imagery, watercolor, markers, colored pencil, 9½ x 16 in. (24.1 x 40.6 cm)

Arlinka Blair, *Medicine Maker*, 2004
Hand-printed and painted paper, 8½ x 16 in.
(21.6 x 40.6 cm)

MY MEMORY DOLL

Bits and pieces of vintage paper doll ephemera and childhood photographs (your own or a stranger's) can be brought together to create a one-of-a-kind paper doll.

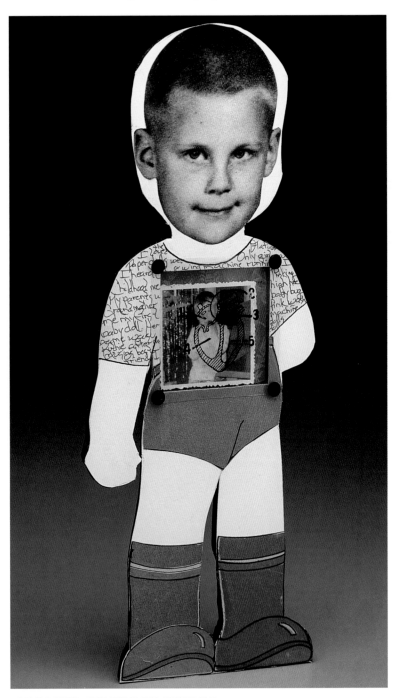

CREATED BY TERRY TAYLOR

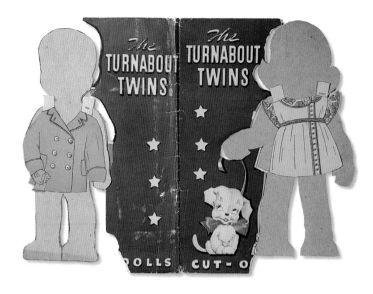

MATERIALS

Foam-core board

Watercolor paper

Spray adhesive

Printable acetate

Clip art

Personal photographs

Paper doll outfits

Fusible interfacing

Stamp pad

Paper fasteners

Vellum

Buttons

1 I asked someone to scan and size a school photograph of mine to fit the cardboard template. I admit it: I'm not digitally savvy. I'm strictly a cut and paste man, but if someone can do it for me, I'm not too proud to beg, if you know what I mean. At the same time, I had childhood photographs of myself scanned and sized to fit in the torso section of the template.

2 I used spray adhesive to mount watercolor paper onto foam-core board. Then I traced the template shape onto the mounted paper and glued my head shot in place.

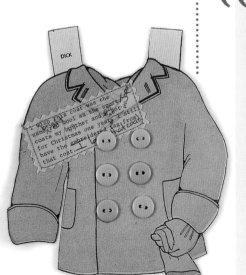

When I began to think about paper dolls before writing this book, I realized that purposeful play with dolls teaches us lessons in cherishing and caring for another. Is that why I enjoyed playing with dolls when I was young?

Something spoke to me when I saw this set online. I wondered: Why did someone make blank cardboard templates of Dick and Sally? Did they make dolls of their own with them? I had no earthly idea what was I going to do with those bits and pieces, but they appealed to me and I had to have them.

The vintage look of Dick's clothing reminded me of my childhood outfits, so I created this biographical piece with family snapshots (yes, that's me and my dolls).
Terry Taylor

3 I cut out several outfits from the set. I glued the shoes and shorts directly onto the figure. The paper was fragile, so I ironed other outfits for my figure on fusible interfacing to strengthen them.

4 I outlined a shirt on the body and wrote biographical snippets on it. Only I know precisely what's written there; the viewer can only guess at the content. Color was added on top of the handwriting with stamping ink. Finally, I used a craft knife to cut a square opening in the torso.

5 I photocopied a medical illustration of a heart onto acetate. I cut out the image slightly larger than the opening in the torso. I punched small holes in each corner of the acetate.

6 I glued a piece of mat board to the back of the figure behind the opening. I used the acetate as a template and drilled matching holes through the foam-core board.

7 Decorative scissors replicated the deckled edges of the original snapshots. I placed them in the opening, then used paper fasteners to attach the acetate to the body.

8 I typed biographical entries onto vellum, cut them apart, then stitched each entry to an outfit. Not satisfied with my writing and typing errors, the editor and ex-educator in me added corrections in red pen. I added buttons to some of the outfits and fashioned a bow tie out of one of Sally's hair bows, just for fun.

Erica Harris, *Toy Theater*, 2002
Rice, paper, collage, thread, acrylic on wood,
24 x 30 x 8 in. (61 x 79.2 x 20.3 cm) PHOTO © ARTIST

Erica Harris, *Auburn Township*, 2005
Collage, eggshells, acrylic on fiberboard,
18 x 24 in. (45.7 x 61 cm) PHOTO © ARTIST

Erica Harris, *Family Portrait*, 2003
Collage, thread, paper on fiberboard,
11 x 17 in. (27.9 x 43.2 cm) PHOTO © ARTIST

Paper Outlaws

Layer upon layer of materials and paint transmogrify the original bases to create these haunting paper dolls.

CREATED BY MICHAEL DE MENG

Paper dolls
Collage elements
Found objects
Glue
Gel medium
Acrylic paints

Only the jointed construction of the original paper dolls is evident after Michael altered them.

1 The bases for Michael's outlaws were vintage, cardboard paper dolls (see photo, top left). In his studio he gathered objects and images (he referred to it as "a large pile of things") that he might or might not use.

2 Michael then "brought out the glue" and started to adhere items. He admits that he's not very tidy with his glue application since he'll alter the piece later to make it appear aged.

3 Collage elements were added after the glue had dried. Michael used gel medium to adhere both photos and text.

4 Michael applied acrylic paint to the piece, tinting objects or adding designs. (In all his work, he experiments with paint as he works.)

5 He added washes to the entire piece to unify disparate objects. He keeps his washes—typically a gold or a black—watery and translucent, adding layer after layer to darken the surface.

6 Once the piece was covered in washes, additional objects and images were added as desired. Additional layers of wash were added as needed.

> **Assemblage and collage** are the perfect allegories for the human existence. One goes though life coming across different ideas, experiences, and beliefs. At some point, these things start to change us and become part of us. My versions of paper dolls are no different. They start with a blank template, but each item added changes it, evolving with time and experience. Paper dolls are reminders of the nature of existence: ever-changing and fragile.
>
> I was inspired by a photograph of the fugitive queen, Belle Starr, posing with her shackled outlaw lover, both living a life fraught with violence and danger. Paper dolls can be viewed as a metaphor for the fragility of life, especially in relation to a violent, fiery one.
>
> We are all paper dolls in a sense. It's just a matter of how close we live to the flame that determines our destiny. Both dolls are adorned with matches, implying that to some degree mortality is within one's control, but never entirely.
> **Michael de Meng**

THE QUEEN OF GAMES

Why stop at making only the queen of games? Create a consort and knave to accompany her royal highness.

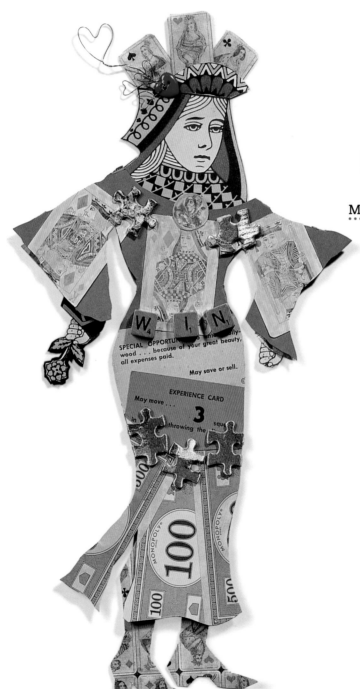

MATERIALS

Playing card

Miniature playing cards

Decorative papers

Card stock

Acrylic paint

1 Lisa photocopied a body template (page 140) to the size she desired. Then she photocopied a queen from a deck of playing cards and enlarged it to match the proportion of her body template. She mounted the photocopied queen onto card stock. She cut out the queen. If the queen needed arms and hands, she drew them on card stock using the queen as a guide.

CREATED BY LISA GLICKSMAN

2 Lisa used the torso photocopy as a template to create the queen's legs and torso from decorative paper. She glued the decorative paper shapes to card stock and attached them to the cut-out queen with glue.

3 She created a crown from miniature playing cards and wove red wire through the punched holes in the crown. Then Lisa glued the crown onto the queen's head.

4 Using the assembled figure as a guide, Lisa sketched out dress shapes onto decorative paper. She made the dresses fit closely by making sure the dress design stayed close to the body at the shoulders, waist, and hips. She added tabs where needed and cut out the dress.

5 Lisa added other elements—collage game pieces (real or photocopied)—and tinted the surfaces with acrylic paint.

6 Lisa created a purse out of a domino. She drilled holes in the domino and threaded wire through the holes to create a strap. A game piece was glued to the top to form a clasp.

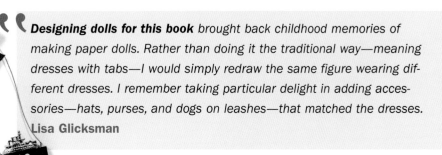

***Designing dolls for this book** brought back childhood memories of making paper dolls. Rather than doing it the traditional way—meaning dresses with tabs—I would simply redraw the same figure wearing different dresses. I remember taking particular delight in adding accessories—hats, purses, and dogs on leashes—that matched the dresses.* **Lisa Glicksman**

QUESTIONING MAN

The plaintive pose of this figure reflects the helpless state of the questioning man. Like Job, with arms raised to the heavens, he asks the questions that have plagued mankind through the ages.

MATERIALS

Poster board
Colored pencils and pens
Metallic markers
Collage elements
Plastic eyeball
Paper fasteners

CREATED BY PAMELA HASTINGS

1 Pamela drew her figure, then transferred the pattern templates (page 142) onto poster board. Pamela used multiple arms to express the helpless feelings or shrug of the arms that accompany the questions that nag us. You may prefer to create a more realistic figure with only two arms and legs.

2 You may wish to adorn the body parts with your own personal questions or images of things that puzzle you. Pamela embellished the individual body parts before cutting them out. She used a combination of colored pencils and pens to add decorative motifs to the parts.

3 Pamela punched holes in the parts, layering the legs together, shortest leg on top, and attached them with a paper fastener. She layered and attached the arms in the same manner.

4 Add a tiny craft eye to your figure as Pamela did.

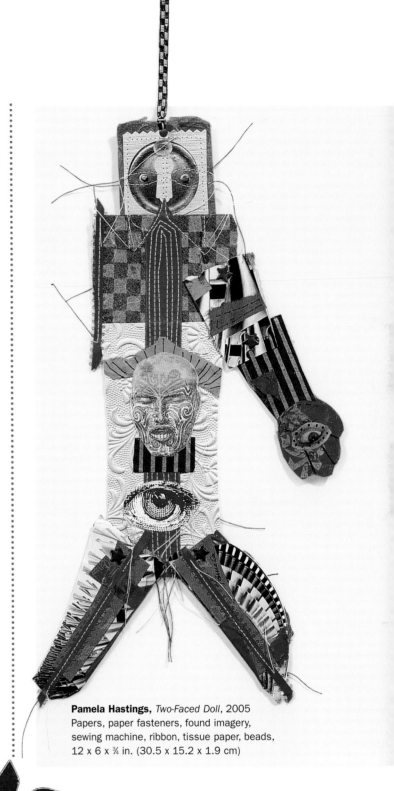

Pamela Hastings, *Two-Faced Doll*, 2005
Papers, paper fasteners, found imagery,
sewing machine, ribbon, tissue paper, beads,
12 x 6 x ¾ in. (30.5 x 15.2 x 1.9 cm)

SECRET MESSAGE DOLL

This doll can function as a secret message board or your own personal shopping list. Draw on her anytime she wants to freshen-up her lipstick or try out a new shade of eye shadow. Sketch lingerie underneath her coat or mesh stockings: She's much more than just a miniature chalkboard.

MATERIALS

Thick cardboard

Black chalkboard paint

Colored chalk or pastels

Crepe paper

Glue

Fur trim

Hot glue

Ribbon

Wire easel

1 Susan painted both sides of thick cardboard with two coats of chalkboard paint. She allowed each coat to dry before adding another coat.

CREATED BY SUSAN MCBRIDE

2 She sketched a simple outline of a figure on the cardboard, then cut it out with a sharp craft knife. Susan touched up the cut edges of the figure with the paint.

3 Susan folded a sheet of crepe paper in half. Using the figure as a guide, she drew a simple coat shape. The neckline and upper edges of the sleeves touched the fold. She cut out the coat, incorporating the neck hole, and cut down the centerline of the coat's front.

4 Susan slipped the coat onto the figure to check the fit. Once she was happy with the fit, she glued the bottom edges of the sleeves and side seams together while the coat remained on the figure.

5 She cut lengths of fur trim for the sleeves and collar and attached them to the coat with hot glue. Susan added a decorative ribbon border to the bottom of the coat. She created a turban of matching ribbon and fur to complete the ensemble.

6 You could make an easel back with a piece of cardboard to allow your doll to stand. Susan chose to display her doll on a wire easel stand.

> **I can recall** receiving paper dolls as gifts for Christmas, and anxiously waiting for my mother (who worked full-time outside the home) to have a spare moment to cut them out for me. Her scissor work was so much neater, and I had butchered enough paper dolls in the past that I knew I preferred her help.
>
> LK Ludwig

A Snippet of History

Newspapers, tabloids, and magazines proliferated in the 1800s. Most of the educated urban populations of Europe and the United States read these new media of mass communication. Magazines, besides featuring serialized fiction and news of the world, instructed their readers in the latest home management techniques, social niceties, and craft techniques, along with drawings of the latest styles of fashionable dress.

Originally, magazines were printed in black and white; color printing came into limited use in the early part of the 19th century. By the 1880s the lithography process and its lush colors was at its zenith, just as photographic methods for reproduction were beginning to evolve. Savvy businesses exploited lithographic printing processes—just as businesses do today with banners on websites—to encourage sales through advertising and promotion. They offered paper premiums in the form of trade cards and sometimes paper dolls. Collectors know that paper premiums were treasured, pasted into albums, and stashed in boxes for safekeeping—you can easily find a surprising number of them today. Fewer advertising paper dolls survive than trade cards, however. It's not difficult to figure out why: they were played with!

In the early 20th century—before radio and television became the dominant modes of communication—advertising meant features in magazines and newspapers. As the century progressed, advertising premiums became less common. However, advertising artists continued to use the paper doll form in a variety of ways.

These late 19th century premiums are ingeniously constructed—the torso is attached separately to each outfit. The Clark's O.N.T. premium offers a complete set of 16 dolls for the price of three 2-cent stamps.

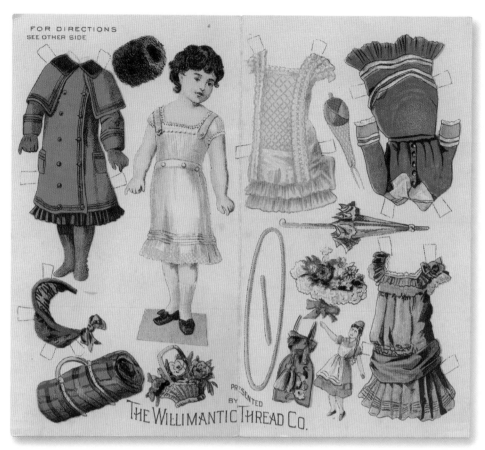

Willimantic Thread Co., late 1800s
FROM THE COLLECTIONS OF THE HENRY FORD MUSEUM (93.0.13.26/G7070)

Americans have associated Little Miss Sunbeam's image with bread since the early 1940s. This premium is an example of modern cross-marketing: It features clothing for the paper doll, in addition to advertising sewing patterns for Mom to duplicate for her little girl. *Quality Bakers of America Cooperative, Inc., 1950*

These late 1940s magazine ads for *Quadriga* cloth—a fine cotton cloth with a needlized finish—featured a future sport legend and a popular film star. Stan Musial—before he became Stan the Man—and his son model outfits made of the cloth. Marilyn Maxwell's ad touts the cloth and recommends the sewing patterns used to create the dresses.

A Dress Is a Dress
Is a Dress

When you're making a paper doll figure, you probably have a vision of what you want it to wear. Or perhaps an image of a dress inspired the figure (see page 22). It doesn't matter what you call the doll's attire: An historical costume, an arty outfit, or a couture frock of your own design. When I think of paper dolls, I think of dresses. So forgive me if I lapse from time to time and refer to an item of attire as a dress when it isn't. You know what I mean.

Paper dolls are traditionally dressed in paper outfits. In general, the dresses are flat, but don't let that constrain your creativity. Create your outfits using any type of paper you like: Handmade paper, crepe and tissue papers, origami or scrapbook papers. If it's paper, use it. There are thousands of beautiful patterned papers to choose from in art and craft stores. You may even be intrigued and inspired to create a doll with scrapbook embellishments. There is a lot of material to choose from to create an outfit.

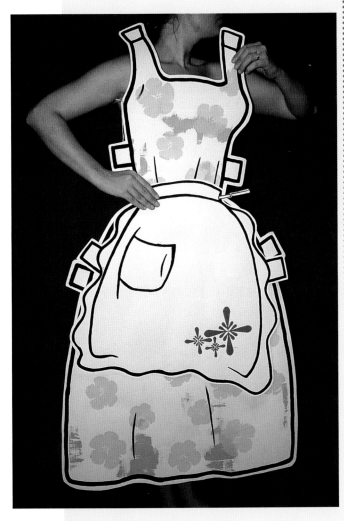

Rebecca Sefcovic Uglem,
*Pink Dress with
Fuchsia Purse*, 2005
Serigraphy on paper,
42⅛ x 24 in.
(107 x 61 cm)
PHOTO © ARTIST;
MODELED BY AMY LYSTE

Rebecca Sefcovic Uglem, *Blue Flower Dress with Apron*, 2004
Serigraphy on paper, 48 x 24 in. (122 x 61 cm)
PHOTO © ARTIST; MODELED BY AMY LYSTE

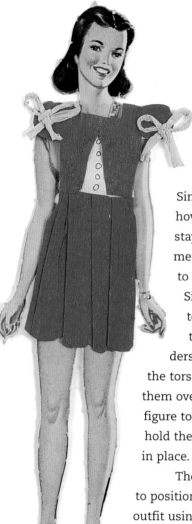

Handmade outfit of crepe paper outfit from the 1940s. *Courtesy of Magnolia Beauregard's Antiques, Asheville, NC*

Since a paper doll is flat, just how will your get the dress to stay on? The time-honored method for attaching a costume to a paper doll is simple tabs. Site the tabs to fit over the shoulders and along the torso. Fold them over the figure to securely hold the costume in place.

The best way to position your tabs is to sketch the outfit using your figure as a guide for size and shape (see page 60). If you find that your costume needs additional tabs after cutting it out and trying it on the doll, simply glue tabs where you want them to the back side of the dress.

From an educational standpoint, there's a logical progression from cutting out paper doll dresses to cutting out patterns from cloth and then sewing a dress.

> *I don't like those little paper flaps that you fold over the body. I hated them as a child. They fall off eventually after being folded back and forth one too many times.*
> **Natascha Luther**

Lots of little girls learned to do so as they grew up. So why not dress your doll with fabric? There's no rule against it. Elinor Peace Bailey dressed her doll in a simple hand-stitched fabric ensemble (page 72). Many of the artists in this book added visual interest to their dolls or dresses with simple hand- or machine-stitching.

Don't think that you have to draw tabs and only tabs on your paper doll outfits. Dresses can be designed to slip over the head in a variety of ways. Slits can be cut in a two-sided outfit and slipped onto the figure. Natascha Luther created an ingeniously constructed figure and using hook-and-loop fasteners to dress her doll in historical costumes (page 64). Eric Allen Montgomery dressed his Reverend Hellfire in paper suits backed with flexible sheet magnets (page 92). Static electricity also can be used to keep costumes in place (see page 17).

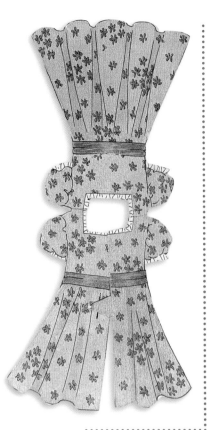

One of the many attractions (if not the attraction) of playing with or creating paper dolls is the wardrobe. It's all about the dresses, you know. One artist created a paper doll dressed in a single outfit (page 102) and others gave in to the joy of making multiple dresses. When I created *My Memory Doll*, I was inspired to use vintage outfits and added embellishments such as stitching and buttons (page 36).

You'll find many different ways to create costumes for your paper dolls in this chapter. Enjoy playing dress up!

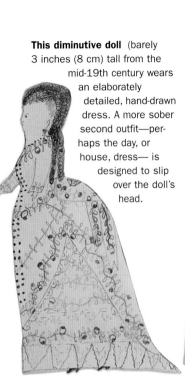

This diminutive doll (barely 3 inches (8 cm) tall from the mid-19th century wears an elaborately detailed, hand-drawn dress. A more sober second outfit—perhaps the day, or house, dress— is designed to slip over the doll's head.

I remember playing with vividly colored Colorforms as opposed to paper dolls. The Colorforms came with a slick cardboard insert that had some type of background scene and figures to be dressed on it. There was a flexible vinyl strip on one side of the board that contained all of the "outfits" and doodads made from a flexible vinyl. You would peel the skirt or pants off of the strip and lay it onto the figure. It magically stayed put, but easily peeled back off. When you changed outfits, you put the pieces back in the right place (there was an outline of each piece). I remember it being a lot of fun. My sister and I both remember having sets inspired by characters from the television shows of the 1960s.

Jean Moore

Fine plaiting, shirring, and ruching are just a few arcane sewing techniques girls used to create the tissue paper costumes pictured in this booklet. Sewing was an important skill to learn and practice. Doll number 9 was single body form. It was created with a separate embossed head which was "gummed" to the body, after a collar was "finely plaited" and "gummed" to it. Separate dress forms with tabs were drawn, cut out, and decorated with tissue and trimmings. The completed dresses were slipped under the collar for a realistic and seamless appearance. *Art and Decoration in Tissue Paper, Dennison Mfg. Company, 1893–1894. Courtesy of Bill Ewald, Argusbooks.com*

Can't you picture this framed, movie star doll hanging in a young girl's room in the 1950s? It's a variation of crafting ribbon art dolls, a popular pastime in the early 20th century (see page 123). Was yellow a favorite color? The figure, a favorite star? Did a young girl make it or did Mother do it for her? Note the construction techniques and materials evident in the back view. The maker used a sheet of printed paper doll outfits to create the base for the skirt.

Lisa Glicksman, *Perpetual Student*, 2006
Mixed media, scissors, wire, 15 x 4 in.
(38 x 10cm)

You could play with these paper dolls while you listened to the music of The Sandpipers and Mitch Miller and Orchestra. 1953, *The Sandpiper Press. Sleeve printed by Western Printing* (see page 16).

"Race against time, cutting out money to outfit your model." Game players mounted the outfits on the plastic "spikes" on these figures. Another clever method of dressing up a doll. *Cut Up Shopping Spree Game, #4980, Milton Bradley, Springfield, Massachusetts, 1969*

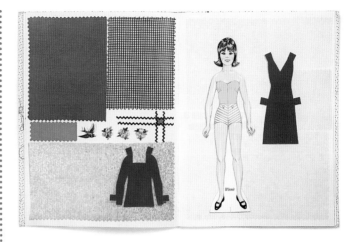

Before decorative scrapbook papers became popular, innovative publishers gave their designers plenty of fashion choices. This book contains stencils for a drop waist dress, A-line skirt, skimmer blouse, capelet, slacks, smart boots, and accessories. Careful instructions are given to punch out the dress patterns ("Be sure not tear the tabs.") and to use the printed trimmings in the book or make your own from leftover scraps.
Winnie's Wardrobe: Doll Book with Stencils,
Whitman Publishing Company, Racine,
Wisconsin, 1966

Printed doll from newspaper comic strip circa 1920s. Who was the budding designer who drew and colored his natty outfits?

ORIGINAL ARTIST
PAPER DOLLS

WRITTEN BY JENNY TALIADOROS

Helen Johnson,
Orange and Lavender, 2005
Photocopy, collage, 10½ x 6 in.
(27 x 15 cm)

Judy M. Johnson, *Art Deco Dollie*, 1992
Colored pencil, 11 x 8½ in.
(28 x 21.5 cm)

When people ask, "What kind of work do you do?" and I reply, "I publish magazines about paper dolls," the response is usually, "I didn't know paper dolls still exist!" Then they want to know how I got into paper dolls in the first place. My answer is, "I was born into it."

I am a third generation paper doll maker. My grandmother, Helen Johnson, collects and makes paper dolls, and my mom, Judy M. Johnson, is a professionally published paper doll artist. So I grew up playing with paper dolls and watching my mom illustrate them.

Today I combine my graphic design skills with my love of paper dolls to produce two magazines. *Paperdoll Review* is a quarterly publication that focuses on the nostalgia of paper dolls. *Paper Doll Studio* is the quarterly magazine for the Original Paper Doll Artists Guild (OPDAG). OPDAG was formed in 1984 to encourage the art and hobby of paper dolls. I take great joy in showcasing paper dolls created by artists from across the country and around the world in these two publications.

The magazines represent both professional and amateur artists. Some are published paper doll artists, some are professionally trained fashion illustrators, and many come from a traditional art background. And there are a number of artists who have no professional training at all but just love to draw paper dolls.

Because publishing opportunities for paper dolls are rare, artists must rely on small paper doll publications, paper doll conventions and their own websites and mailing lists to let people know about their art. Our publications accept paper dolls by all the artists who submit—no one is rejected. Our theme-based issues inspire artists to create paper dolls that cover a wide variety of subjects and fashion eras.

Two methods are commonly used to create finished paper dolls pages. Both involve drawing preliminary sketches and transferring those sketches to a final page. One of two methods uses tracing paper, the other uses a light box.

Using a No. 2 pencil, a figure is drawn on a tracing paper, such as parchment or vellum. Knowledge of figure drawing is helpful in illustrating an anatomically believable doll. There are numerous books on the topic of figure drawing. I find that the out-of-print books by Andrew Loomis are especially useful. Current and vintage magazines are a great resource for ideas for both figures and poses. Many paper doll artists keep clip files of poses, arms, legs, and hands for reference.

After the figure is sketched, it's time to create a costume for the doll. To ensure a good fit, another piece of tracing paper must to be placed on top of the figure and the outfit sketched with a No. 2 pencil. Use a separate piece of tracing paper for each outfit. Tabs are added at strategic points so the costume doesn't fall off.

All of the sketches are transferred to bristol board. A popular transfer method uses handmade graphite paper. This is done by taking a blank piece of tracing paper and rubbing a soft pencil over it until it is covered. Unlike the commercial carbon paper, transfers from handmade graphite paper are easily erased.

Since the doll and outfits are sketched on separate pieces of tracing paper, you can move them around on the bristol board to create different types of layouts. The tracing paper is secured with artist's tape on the board, the graphite paper slipped in between the sketch and the board, and a sharp fine point pencil is used to trace over the lines.

After the sketches are transferred the images must be finalized. To do this, draw over the transferred lines with permanent ink. If a mistake occurs in the inking process, correction fluid comes in handy. If the final piece will be in color, a colored pencil may be used instead of an ink pen for drawing the outline. Finally, use a soft eraser to remove any uninked graphite lines.

For final coloring, you can use most any medium such as watercolor, gouache, water-soluble colored pencils, or markers. Tempera or poster paint may be used to achieve special effects. Background painting, page decorations, and lettering are often added to complete the page layout.

Some artists prefer to sketch on paper that's heavier

Norma Lu Meehan, *The Days of John Singer Sargent*, 2005
Watercolor, 11 x 8½ in. (28 x 21.5 cm)

than tracing paper. Photocopy paper is often used because of its smooth surface and availability. Because this paper is opaque, a strong light source is needed to see through for doing costume designs and the final transfer to bristol paper.

Like the graphite transfer method, the initial sketches are done on separate pieces of paper. This time, the sketches are put down on a light box with bristol board on top. The designs are traced with a No. 2 pencil on the bristol. The next steps are the same: Inking over the pencil, erasing the pencil lines, and adding color.

There's really no right or wrong way to do paper doll art, but creating clean work, costumes that fit, and a pleasing layout are important factors.

My favorite part of paper doll art is the creative expression. Some paper dolls showcase skillfully rendered costumes, others are simply cleverly or amusingly designed. And I love the way paper dolls represent different aspects of fashion. Our history is intertwined with the clothing worn through decades and centuries gone by. I hope artists will continue to capture the glorious fashion eras of the past and forecast what is to come in the future through the art of the paper doll.

Kwei-lin Lum, Isabelle and Chloe—Trapped in Skoo, 2004
Computer-assisted illustration printed on acid-free cardstock, 11 x 8½ in. (27.9 x 21.6 cm)

KATY KEENE

A DIFFERENT DOLL

Katy Keene was a different sort of paper doll. Not only did she have a comic book that brought her to life through high-profile adventures, she also wore dazzling clothes designed by her dutiful fans. Thousands of girls and boys from around the nation sent in glamorous gowns, down-to-earth dresses, sportswear, scarves, shoes, jewelry, hats, and even cars for the outgoing pinup paper doll to incorporate into her fashionable lifestyle. Katy's creator, William Woggon, first drew her for his *Archie* comic. She appeared as a peripheral character between 1945 and 1949, when she finally got her own title. Unlike most comics of the time, Katy Keene deviated from stories of espionage, the Wild West, and super-heroes to focus primarily on

HUDSON, INS, NG, SYLVANIA. AIL FORTUNE, 131 ELLAN CLAIRE, SAN ANTONIO, TEXAS, (AGE 12)

fashion. Woggon tried to use as many of the fan's designs as possible, so Katy rarely stayed in one outfit for more than a page. And of course, readers were given the additional luxury of dressing Katy in any of the several cut-out ensembles at the end of each issue.

Katy Keene was a huge commercial success. At the height of the series' popularity, each installment sold over a million copies. Because of reader enthusiasm for the paper doll aspect of the comic, however, it is very difficult to find intact copies today. However, her popularity did spawn non-doll spin-off titles such as *Katy Keene Pinup Parade, Katy Keene Annual, Katy Keene Glamour, Katy Keene Charm, and Katy Keene Spectacular,* all of which may be easier to find in one piece.

The girls' comic trend came to an end after a decade of distinction. In the face of declining readership, Woggon received word on April 15, 1961, to stop work on Katy Keene. The comic's popularity throughout the 1950s, however, left a lasting impression. Several contemporary fashion designers, including Betsey Johnson, Willie Smith, and Anna Sui, have acknowledged Katy Keene's seminal role in inspiring their creativity.

In 1978, after Saks Fifth Avenue in New York City used Katy Keene covers as a backdrop for a window display, the comic experienced a resurgence of public attention. Katy conventions, newsletters, and fanzines abounded. Between 1983 and 1990 a new Katy Keene comic appeared regularly, featuring Woggon reprints as well as new material. Today, *Archie Comics* artist John Lucas continues to draw Katy for the occasional paper doll project, and fans continue to enjoy dressing her in the clothes they design.

CAVALCADE OF HISTORICAL COSTUMES

It's said that the devil is in the details. From the tiny slippers to the ringlets attached to the hats, the attention to detail in this remarkable collection is worth emulating.

CREATED BY NATASCHA LUTHER

Card stock

Cardboard

Acrylic paints

Iridescent acrylic paint

Rubber stamps

Stamping inks

Hook-and-loop tape

Paper fasteners

1 Natascha scanned a template on page 140 and printed it on card stock. To give the doll more body, she glued the card stock to a heavier cardboard. She slightly adjusted the waist and hips.

2 Natascha gave careful thought to how her doll's body would move freely when dressed. She decided to fix arms to both sleeves for every costume. Because Natascha dislikes tabs (see page 54), she decided to place a corset-shape piece of hook-and-loop tape on the torso and the bodice of each costume part.

3 The doll parts were colored with acrylic paint and given features before Natascha attached the corset shape to the torso with glue. She didn't want her doll to look underdressed without her outfits, so she created a simple chemise shape

4 Natascha studied an encyclopedia of historical costume and sketched the dresses she was going to make. To make a final pattern, she traced the outline of her doll and sketched a costume directly on the traced figure. She sketched one sleeve over one arm template.

5 Natascha prepared card stock for each dress by painting it with acrylic and iridescent paints. She stamped each dried base coat with patterned rubber stamps. You might choose to use patterned card stock, scanned fabric, or scrapbook papers to create your costumes.

6 The costume sketch and arm became patterns that Natascha traced onto the cardstock. To make the opposite arm Natascha simply flipped the sleeve template. She added skin tone to each hand with acrylic paint.

7 Natascha assembled the costumes with paper fasteners. She attached a matching hook and loop corset shape to the back of each costume.

8 Hats were made in the same fashion as the costumes using sketches as patterns. Natascha made tiny curls of hair with thin strips of colored paper rolled around a toothpick. A slit was cut into the hat to fit atop the head.

9 Historical fashion dictates that not every outfit needs a matching pair of shoes. At different times in history it was considered imprudent (if not immoral) to expose the foot. Why bother giving every doll a pair of shoes if they won't be visible? If your costume needs a pair of shoes, add hook- and-loop tape to each foot and shoe.

10 Use decorative paper punches to make lacey trims for the dresses. Natascha cut the decorative bows, ribbons, and trimmings freehand.

> **I sew full-sized historic costumes** for myself. This gives me insights into the different aspects of fashion design and construction through the ages. When I was asked to make a paper doll, I imagined a doll with dresses from different time periods—from the medieval through the baroque, Regency, and Edwardian periods.
> **Natascha Luther**

Margi Hennen, *The Queen of Spades*, 2005
Playing card, paper, brad, found imagery,
13 x 4¾ in. (33 x 12 cm)
PHOTO © DANNY ABRIEL

Kathryn Belzer, *Flipping King*, 2005
Old playing card, advertisement clippings,
3½ x 2½ in. (8.9 x 6.4 cm) PHOTO © DANNY ABRIEL

Jacqueline Meyers-Cho, *J*, 2005
Cardboard, photocopies, stencil, muslin, fiberfill,
8 x 6½ in. (20 x 17 cm)

ÉCOLE DES BEAUX-ARTS POUPÉE

The rich detail of vintage architectural renderings inspired this doll. You could describe her as statuesque, perhaps, or as a pillar of society.

CREATED BY SHANNON YOKELEY

Computer

Clip art

Poster board

Spray adhesive

Paper fasteners

1 Shannon scanned and imported architectural clip art illustrations from various sources.

2 Shannon scanned the template on page 140 and imported both the illustrations and template into a layout or desktop publishing program. Using the layout program, she moved images onto template parts, looking for the best fit: A column for a leg or arm, classical sculpture for the head.

3 Using the template as a guide, she sized elements such as the dome and the capital of a column to use as clothing. Rather than add tabs, she planned to cut slits into the shapes to slip them onto the figure.

4 When she was satisfied with all the parts, Shannon printed out the images, then mounted them onto poster board before cutting them out.

5 Shannon used paper fasteners to connect the body parts. She used a sharp craft knife to cut slits into the imagery used for the outfits.

> **I work on a computer** most every day as an art director. I enjoy how the computer has replaced labor-intensive cut-and-paste methods. Terry asked for a doll composed of classical architectural elements and I gave him exactly what he wanted. Didn't I?
> **Shannon Yokeley**

HENRY GELDZAHLER'S PAPER DOLLS

Dress your dolls in Pollock frocks or Mondrian mini-skirts. Give them tribal heads, Titian tresses, or armorial appendages. Play fast and loose with the richness of art's history.

CREATED BY MAR GOMAN

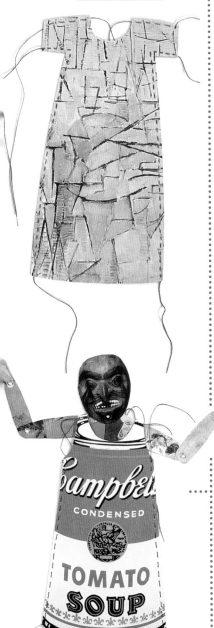

MATERIALS

Art history books
Eyelets and setting tools
Glue stick

1 Mar began making her dolls by first finding heads and hands in her art history books. She cut them out and photocopied them, enlarging or reducing them as she wished.

2 You can adapt any of the templates in this book to create your own art dolls; Mar designed her own. Simply enlarge or reduce a template to fit under your doll's head. You can follow the seven-and-a-half rule (page 12) or, better yet, follow your own instincts.

Once Mar selected the art she wished to use for the body of the dolls, she transferred the template parts to the back of the selected pages. She carefully wrote the name of the artist and title of the piece she had chosen on the reverse side of each piece.

3 The body parts were joined with eyelets, taking care to set the eyelets firmly enough that the joints move, but not too easily. A simple way to do this is to slip a scrap of paper between the parts to be joined, set the eyelet, and then carefully remove the scrap of paper.

4 Mar traced a dress shape around each figure on a piece of paper, then transferred the shape to selected pages. She cut out two pieces and dabbed a tiny amount of glue along the edges to hold the two together. This makes stitching along the edges a much easier process. Mar left the thread ends dangling as a decorative touch.

5 As for the title of her project, Mar and I emailed back and forth: I suggested H. W. Janson's dolls (Janson, the author of *History of Art*); Mar countered with Lee Krasner's or Gertrude Stein's dolls. Finally, we both agreed that Henry Geldzahler (1935–1994), a colorful art critic and collector of 1960s pop art, might have approved of her appropriations.

❝❝**When I went through art school** *years ago, I accumulated a lot of art history books. As time passed, these books interested me less and less, and in recent years I've taken to cutting them up to use in my own work. In fact, I now purchase art books at used bookstores exclusively to cut up.*
Mar Goman ❞❞

OLD WOMAN IN PURPLE

Here's your chance to make an outrageously colorful outfit for a doll.
Just follow elinor's sage advice.

MATERIALS

Watercolor paper
Colored pencils
Watercolors
Lightweight fabrics
Lace
Needle and thread
Brads
Beads
Craft wire
Hair
Miniature doll
Miniature bow
Miniature purse

1 elinor created her figure in the style of a pantin. She drew features on her figure and added bright coloring with colored pencils. Use her figure's template (page 141) as a guide for your own version of this doll. Enlarge the template and transfer the shapes to watercolor paper. Add features of your choice using any of the suggested techniques on page 14. Cut out the template pieces and assemble the arms and legs with brads to allow movement. Attach the legs to the torso, but don't attach the arms.

CREATED BY ELINOR PEACE BAILEY

2 elinor made a pattern for a simple sleeveless dress to fit her figure. Using very lightweight fabric, she cut out two shapes, and then stitched them together. She slipped the dress onto the torso and then attached the arms.

She stitched tubes out of knit fabric to serve as sleeves and slipped the sleeves onto the arms, tucking them into the dress.

3 elinor wears glasses, so she wanted her doll to have them too. She fashioned a small pair of glasses out of craft wire, styled the doll with a lock of real hair (why not use your own?), and added other embellishments to the hat.

4 After the doll was dressed and accessorized, elinor wrapped a yarn boa around the neck. If you peeked underneath her dress (and I did!), you'd find a dainty, purple lace slip.

Arlinka Blair, *Behold*, 2005
Found imagery from magazines, printed cardboard paper, banana leaf, ink markers, 11 x 14 in. (27.9 x 35.6 cm)

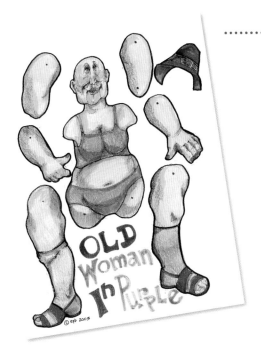

❝ ***Everyone loves a wise old woman.*** *They always come into your life at just the right moment and put it all in perspective. They've always suffered more than you have and have more aches and pains, but they're still planning for the future! So dress them in something comfortable and bright. Listen to their stories and weave them into your life.*
elinor peace bailey ❞

STITCHED PAPER DOLLIES

You'll be amazed at the wonderful patterns you can make with simple, straight stitches. The weight of handmade paper makes it an ideal surface for stitching on. Don't be afraid of stitching on paper, it's a breeze. (Just remember not to pull your stitches too tightly!)

MATERIALS

Handmade papers

Waxed linen, embroidery floss, sewing threads

Tapestry needle

Awl

Buttons, beads, or other embellishments

Glue

Waxed paper

CREATED BY CLAUDIA LEE

1   You may wish to use the trick of folding a sheet of paper in half to make a symmetrical figure (page 12) or use a simple cookie cutter template. Claudia drew a simple doll pattern on mat board and cut it out. Then she traced her pattern onto paper and cut out a body for each doll.

2   Claudia drew a simple dress pattern to fit each doll. She cut out two matching dresses for each doll, which later would be glued back to back.

3   Next, she glued small shapes of paper— decorative details such as pockets, aprons, or trim—onto the dresses.

4   Claudia placed a dress form on a safe surface—a magazine or piece of foam core board—and used an awl to punch holes in the dress for stitching.
She used simple straight stitches and a variety of threads to embellish the dresses. You can stitch or glue beads, buttons, or sequins to the dress as well.

5   Next, she spread a thin coat of glue on the back side of each matching dress shape. Then she sandwiched the body between the matched forms.

6   She wrapped the doll between two pieces of waxed paper, placed a heavy book on top, and allowed it to dry thoroughly.

> **When I was a child, I** had a great interest in anything paper, but the idea of cutting out paper dolls was too exacting for me. I was definitely an "outside the lines" artist. When I tried to cut out paper dolls and their clothes, the clothes wouldn't ever fit. So, while I owned books of paper dolls (which I enjoyed very much), I never cut them out. I just treated them like any other book and pulled them out to look at.
> **Claudia Lee**

SUNDAY BEST DRESS

A sheet of vintage paper doll dresses inspired this sculptural version of a paper doll dress. Folding the individual pleats makes it a standout work of art.

CREATED BY JEAN TOMASO MOORE

MATERIALS

Vintage paper doll dresses

Decorative scrapbook papers

Card stock

Paper doilies, vellum, or other decorative papers

Foam-core board

Embroidery and sewing thread

Vintage buttons, ribbons, lace, trims, old wristwatch band (used as belt), other embellishments

Shadow box frame

1 Jean enlarged (no larger than 12 x 12 inches [30 x 30 cm]) and photocopied one of the dresses from a page of uncut paper doll outfits. She made several copies, cut out one complete outfit, then cut apart the separate components of the outfit: jacket, skirt, and blouse. Then Jean went shopping for coordinating, decorative papers.

2 Jean used the cut-out components as templates. With a pencil, she traced around each template onto the scrapbook papers.

3 Using the complete outfit (including the tabs) as a template, Jean traced the shape onto the foam-core board. She used a craft knife to cut out the shape.

4 Then, she stitched along the folded lines of the pink jacket to make it appear more realistic. You could also draw stitched lines with a marker. She added a paper lace collar.

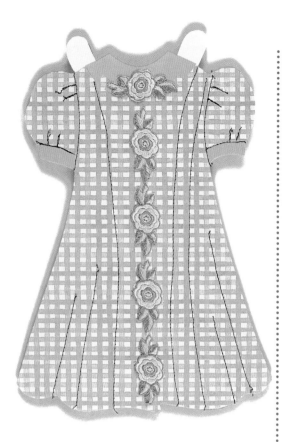

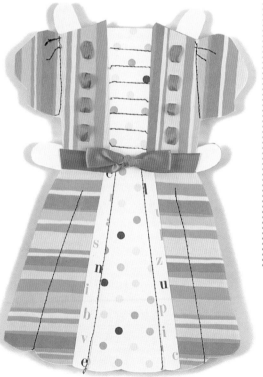

5 For the blouse, Jean used white cardstock overlaid with printed vellum. She hand stitched buttons to the blouse and glued the blouse to the foam-core base.

6 Jean folded back the jacket fronts to add dimension to the piece and glued only the jacket's sleeves to the base. She glued small blocks of foam-core board under each jacket front to prevent them from falling flat.

7 Next, she cut the skirt shape from decorative paper and glued it to the foam-core base. She drew a triangular shape on matching decorative paper, cut off the point, and folded it to create a pleat. Double-sided tape was used to secure the pleat in place on the skirt. She made additional pleats to cover the skirt.

8 Jean photocopied the sheet of paper doll dresses and used the photocopies to line the interior and back of the shadow box. Rickrack trim was added to the edge of the shadow box for a special retro touch.

Karen L. Shelton, *Search for Clues*, 2004
Magazine images, white glue, playing card, wallpaper samples,
permanent marker, rubber stamping, stickers, 12¾ x 8 in. (30 x 20 cm)

Karen L. Shelton, (left to right) *Think Pink* and *Scenic Route*, 2004
Magazine images, white glue, hand colored photocopies, stickers,
each 12¾ x 8 in. (30 x 20 cm)

What's In Your Closet?

Create a closetful of cards to give to friends and family.
It's an ingenious (and impressive)
way to play dress up.

MATERIALS

Paper doll dresses

Spray adhesive

Heavy weight paper
such as card stock or
watercolor paper

Scrapbook
embellishments

Miniature wire hanger
or craft wire

CREATED BY TERRY TAYLOR

1   I selected larger than usual vintage paper doll dresses for this project. The dresses—made for a large doll—are approximately 7 inches (18cm) tall.

2   Next, I mounted each dress on heavy paper using spray adhesive. I find that spray adhesive works well when you are gluing fragile vintage papers.

3   I folded the paper in half to form a card, making sure the fold was near the top of each tab. Using a sharp craft knife, I cut around each tab and the neckline through both layers. I cut out the two layers of the card around the dress, leaving the shoulder area at the fold uncut. On the back side, I cut off the tab shapes.

4   At the top of each shoulder or sleeve I carefully folded back the fold. Then I opened the card and tucked the center fold down behind the sleeve. In origami, that sort of fold is called a valley fold. I trimmed away any of the fold that stuck out from the sleeve. To finish the card, I put a dab of glue inside the valley fold and placed the card flat under a heavy book to dry.

5   Add your own simple dimensional elements to each dress: a paper flower, a jeweled locket, floral sequins.

6   If you can't find miniature wire hangers in your local craft store, use a heavy gauge of craft wire to create your own. Simply sketch a hanger in the size you need, and use your fingers or pliers to bend the wire to shape.

When this book was opened, a fully furnished house popped up. An entire paper doll family and wardrobe made this a toy to be envied. *Dolls' Open House, Platt & Munk Publishers, New York 10, NY, 1963. Collection of Suzie Million$*

It's 3-Dimension Magic!

DOLLS'
OPEN
HOUSE

Mom, Dad, Brother, Sister
Wardrobes to Cut Out
~Furniture~
COMPLETE

PLATT & MUNK
Publishers

A Snippet of History

It's uncommon, but not unheard of, for paper dolls to come replete with an environment or a specially created space for storage. As children, we created our own imaginary environments as we played with paper dolls. I remember sitting on a narrow staircase in my grandparents' house, playing paper dolls with my cousin and pretending each step was a separate apartment. I don't remember how we stored those paper dolls. Was it in an envelope or tucked between the pages of a magazine?

On rare occasions, commercially made paper doll sets in the 19th and 20th centuries included flat printed patterns to cut out and assemble into dimensional furniture. More common, but still rare, is flat cardboard furniture with slits marked for cutting. Dolls were slipped into the cut slits of a crib, changing table, or playpen.

> *My mother sewed a lot*, and occasionally she brought home one of those big pattern books from a fabric store. I loved to cut out the figures and their clothes from those books. They were far superior to mail-order catalogs, which were our other source of free paper dolls. Of course, using the catalogs, you could provide your doll family with everything they needed, right down to sofas and kitchen appliances.
>
> **Mar Goman**

Even rarer are pop-up houses, complete with a paper doll family. Vintage craft books and craft magazines for children frequently featured patterns and instructions for making paper furniture out of flat sheets of paper or recycled cardboard boxes. However, enterprising children often took matters into their own hands when it came to creating unique homes for their paper dolls.

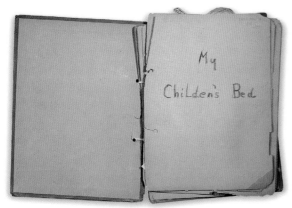

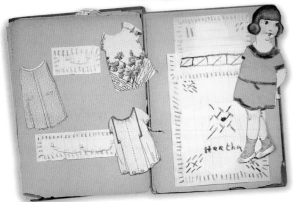

The child who created *My Childen's Bed* for these dolls, carefully created pocket-like beds of blue-lined notebook paper. Each bed is individually embellished with crayons for one paper doll to be tucked into. Simple strips on the facing page function as closets to hold the doll's wardrobe.

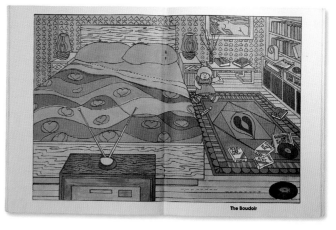

This groovy boudoir features dotted lines on the waterbed to be cut before slipping in the swinging paper doll figures. *The Official Hunks Paper Doll Book,* Pocket Books, New York, New York, 1984

A House Is a Home

It's great fun to create a special environment—a home if you will—for paper dolls. A home can be as simple as a hand-lettered envelope used to hold the figure and outfits (page 11) or as complex as your imagination envisions and your hands create. An environment gives added meaning and context for a viewer looking at your artful paper doll creations. By placing your dolls in an environment they become much more than simple playthings.

A well-made figure or imaginative clothing forms are interesting in and of themselves. Natascha Luther's paper doll (page 64) doesn't need an environment for anyone to "get it." When I began working on Madam I'm Adam (page 96), I knew that a lone, naked figure wasn't enough, even if I made an interesting wardrobe. How would anyone looking at the figure know it was Adam? Could I make a small, removable fig leaf for the figure? To give the figure context and meaning for the viewer, I knew I had to create an environment for him. Once I created a garden for Adam (and figured out how to give him a removable fig leaf), the piece came together.

In this chapter, you'll see how different artists created interesting and unusual environments for their paper dolls. A home for a paper doll can be as simple as an

Jack and Jill, May, 1960, *The Curtis Publishing Company, Philadelphia, Pennsylvania*

envelope. (Make it after you finish making the doll; you want the doll to fit inside it, don't you?) Use interesting papers and collage materials to create a rustic, urban, or a totally imaginary environment. Mount the papers on a mat board to give them strength.

Frame your paper doll, but create a unique background for it with collage, drawing, or patterned papers. If you want to add dimension to the piece, choose a shadow box instead of a flat frame. Placing objects in the frame and mounting your dolls on thick materials will give dimension to your paper dolls (page 86).

Simple pocket forms (not unlike pocket beds) are very easy to construct. Simply join two pieces of paper with glue, brads, tape, stitching, or staples. Make a pocket plain and simple or artfully embellished as Lina Olson did (page 90). Collaged tins or paperboard boxes make beautiful homes for paper dolls (page 98). Book forms, as you'll learn in the next chapter, are still another intriguing way to create an environment for your paper dolls.

James Michael Starr, *Whom the Father Has Chastened*, 2001
Wood box, book pages, photographic print, starfish, coin bank, balls of various materials, watch part, epoxy, ink, 12¼ x 9 x 3½ in. (31 x 23 x 9 cm)
PHOTO © HARRISON EVANS

Bob's Paper Doll Party

Just a small amount of text explains Bob's solemn look and sets up a wonderful story. Poor Bob, he didn't realize what fun he was missing.

MATERIALS

Photocopied photographs

Medium weight watercolor paper

Colored pencils, pastels, and acrylic paints

Glue

Acrylic medium

Small blocks of wood

Shadow box

CREATED BY MADONNA PHILLIPS

1 Madonna enlarged and photocopied vintage photographs. She mounted them on watercolor paper and cut them out.

2 Using the cut-out figures as guides, she drew outfits on watercolor paper. She added tabs to each outfit.

3 Madonna used a variety of coloring tools to embellish and add text to the outfits. The finished outfits were glued to the figures.

4 Colors and text were added to a piece of watercolor paper that Madonna cut to fit inside her shadow box. Elements of landscape were added to give the figures a grounded space.

5 The figures were glued to small blocks of wood to make them stand away from the background.

6 Small house shapes were sawn out of wood. Madonna painted them, then lettered them to spell out "paper."

7 The mounted figures were glued to the background. The houses were glued to the lower inside edge of the shadow box. Madonna then placed the background inside the frame.

Erica Harris, *If You See Something, Say Something*, 2005
Collage, sewing pattern, paper acrylic on fiberboard, 16 x 24 in. (40.6 x 61 cm)
PHOTO © ARTIST

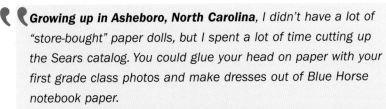

> **Growing up in Asheboro, North Carolina**, *I didn't have a lot of "store-bought" paper dolls, but I spent a lot of time cutting up the Sears catalog. You could glue your head on paper with your first grade class photos and make dresses out of Blue Horse notebook paper.*
>
> *My mother used to say, "You're going to pick up every giblet (she called little shards of paper giblets) of that cut up paper on the hardwood floor." I was thinking the other day that I've sort of made a career out of cutting up paper.*
> **Madonna Phillips**

HAPPY HOLDEN'S PLAYHOUSE

Here's a clever take on a traditional form. Who would have imagined that a paper doll chain could become so elaborate?

CREATED BY LINA TRUDEAU OLSON

Photo

Clip art

Colored pencils

Acrylic medium

Acrylic paint

Heavy paper

Collage elements

Eyelets and setting tools

Ribbons, feathers, and other embellishments.

1 Lina proposed that she make a contemporary paper doll chain. She posed her son—arms akimbo—specifically to create the doll form. She printed the photos, choosing to print some in reverse.

2 Using a desktop publishing program, Lina used the photo as a template to size her selected clip art outfits. She superimposed the clip art images on the photos to make sure they fit, then printed them out.

3 Lina colored each outfit with colored pencil, then glazed each outfit with acrylic medium. To unify the stylistic differences in the costumes, she glazed them with a wash of acrylic. Lina cut out the clothing and glued each outfit onto a photo.

4 Next, Lina laid her figures in a line, and created long strips of sturdy paper to create a base for the figures and to connect them elbow to elbow. She collaged words related to costuming, play, and dress up to the strips. You could use plain or decorative paper for strips; just be sure it is sturdy enough to stand unsupported.

> **My son loves to play dress-up.** He spends a lot of time imagining himself as a hero or a great adventurer. His love of dramatic play, of all things "pretend," and costuming are my inspiration for this paper doll series.
> **Lina Trudeau Olson**

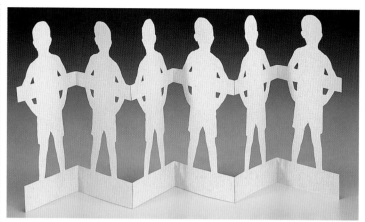

5 Lina glued the figures on the strips, spacing them to allow room to accordion fold the figures. She placed the figures between sheets of waxed paper, weighted them with books, and allowed them to dry overnight.

6 After the figures dried, Lina collaged words on the reverse side of both the connecting strips and figures. She allowed the assembly to dry overnight between sheets of waxed paper.

7 Lina created a playhouse-shape pocket for the figures. She collaged playful phrases— "Come Play with Me," "Walk the Plank," and "Put 'Em Up"—onto the roof and the front pocket and added ribbon trim. She connected the front to the back with eyelets and hung miniature toys along the bottom edge.

Gwendolyn McLarty, *Paradise Lost–Removable Story Rings
with Interchangeable Parts*, 2005
Assembled images, copper, cement, mirrors, fish hook, thread,
mica, steel, 24-karat gold leaf, architectural greenery, 9 x 7⅛ x 5 in.
(23 x 18 x 12.8 cm) PHOTO © JACK ZILKER

Nicole McConville, *Girl*, 2003
Wooden frame, photo, found writing, anatomical illustration, paper,
beeswax, clock gear, tree bark, plastic, 6¼ x 6½ x 2 in.
(15.9 x 16.5 x 5.1 cm) PHOTO © STEVE MANN

Julie Fillo, *Beach Girl Cigar Box Assemblage*, 2005
Cigar box, handmade paper doll, plastic lid, acrylic paints, original photo, shells,
glue, brads, rubber stamps, 9 x 13 x 1½ in. (23 x 33 x 4 cm) PHOTO © DAVE FILLO

Hellfire's Marvelous Medicine Show

This project was difficult to pigeonhole into a chapter. The outfits were ingeniously made and the environment was created with an unusual choice of materials. The question is: Which came first, the outfits or the environment? Only the artist knows for sure.

CREATED BY ERIC ALLEN MONTGOMERY

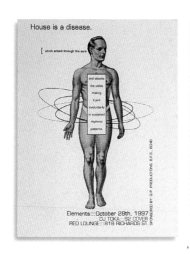

MATERIALS

- Cabinet photo
- Vintage imagery
- Sheet magnet
- Rare-earth magnets
- Spray adhesive
- Balsa or thin plywood
- Vintage books and papers
- Clear adhesive film
- Mat acrylic medium
- Acrylic paint
- Flame stencil
- Steel baking sheet
- Frame
- Heavy-duty glue
- Charms, milagros, miniature bottles

> " **I first found Hellfire's image** several years ago. I imagined him as a fire and brimstone type evangelist. While digging through my vintage paper scraps for "clothing" materials, I rediscovered a long forgotten 1900s State of California business license issued to Marvel Remedies. Hellfire's true vocation as a seller of miracle cures was born. Caveat emptor! "
>
> **Eric Allen Montgomery**

1 Eric scanned and sized a vintage anatomical illustration on an invitation and the cabinet photo. Though he admits to generally relying on scissors and glue technologies, he does have some basic computer skills. After printing out several copies of the images, he relied on cut-and-paste techniques to adjust the position of the figure's arms.

2 To give dimension to the figure, Eric mounted the head onto a small piece of thin wood, cut it out, and mounted a rare-earth magnet on the back of the head. (Rare-earth magnets are stronger than the sheet magnet and are better suited to holding items on a vertical surface.) Then he glued the body to sheet magnet with spray adhesive.

3 Eric created templates for Hellfire's many outfits (far more than those shown here) by tracing the outline of the body and transferring the shapes to the clear adhesive film. He then adhered a variety of vintage papers to the shapes and roughly cut them out. The clear adhesive film gave the outfits a shiny plastic look. Using spray adhesive, he adhered them to sheet magnet and trimmed them neatly.

4 Stenciled flame motifs were added to the back of the baking sheet with acrylic paint. Once the paint was dry, Eric used heavy-duty glue to adhere the baking sheet inside the frame.

5 Eric scanned and reduced a variety of vintage paper items, including the Marvel Remedies business license. Rare-earth magnets were attached to various charms, bottles, and milagros with heavy-duty glue. The vintage paper items were glued to sheet magnet with spray adhesive.

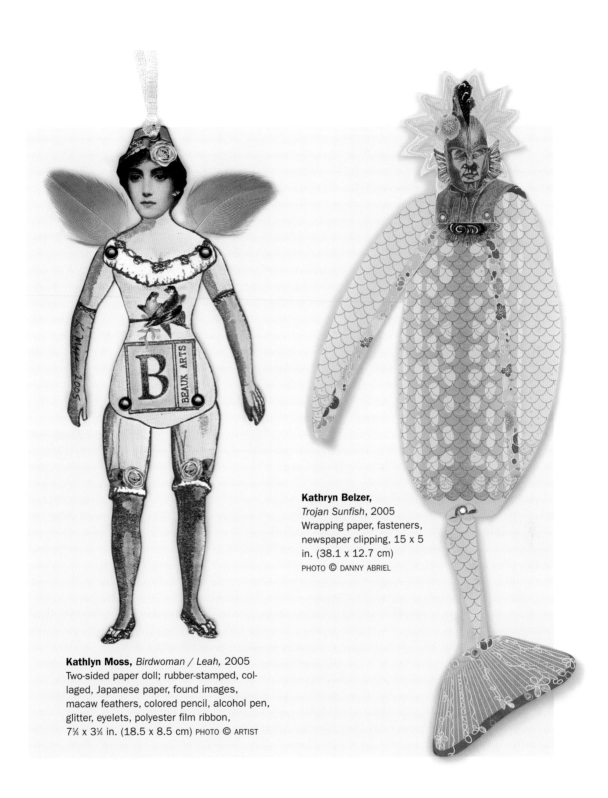

Kathlyn Moss, *Birdwoman / Leah,* 2005
Two-sided paper doll; rubber-stamped, collaged, Japanese paper, found images,
macaw feathers, colored pencil, alcohol pen,
glitter, eyelets, polyester film ribbon,
7¼ x 3¼ in. (18.5 x 8.5 cm) PHOTO © ARTIST

Kathryn Belzer,
Trojan Sunfish, 2005
Wrapping paper, fasteners,
newspaper clipping, 15 x 5
in. (38.1 x 12.7 cm)
PHOTO © DANNY ABRIEL

Madam, I'm Adam

After I created this paper doll, this prime example of a palindrome came immediately to mind. Let's face it, it's more appropriate than "Selma, I am Les."

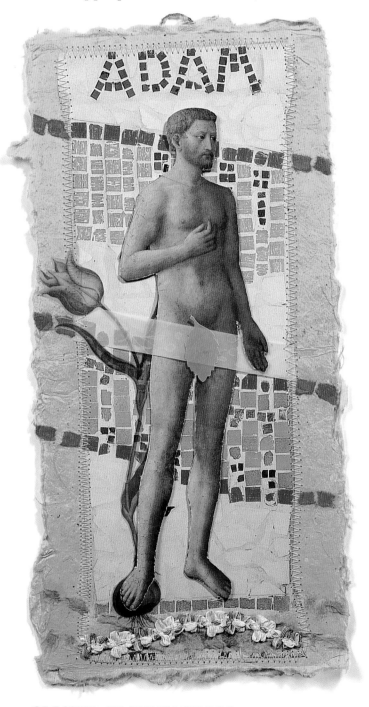

And the eyes of both of them were opened, and they knew that they were naked; and they sewed fig leaves together, and made themselves aprons.

And he said, I heard thy voice in the garden, and I was afraid, because I was naked; and I hid myself.

And he said, Who told thee that thou wast naked?

Genesis 3:7,10,11

CREATED BY TERRY TAYLOR

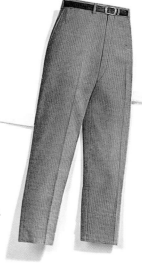

MATERIALS

Handmade paper

Decorative papers

Collage materials

Glue

Card stock

Ribbon

Glassine envelope

Mat board

Acrylic medium

1 I cut out Adam—Eve was partially hidden behind the tree—and mounted him on heavy card stock. I tinted the edges of the cardstock with rubber-stamp ink.

2 Poring over men's fashion magazines, catalogs, and a vintage mail-order catalog, I found outfits that would fit the figure. A plaid skirt became a kilt with the addition of a little bag. Each article of clothing was cut out and mounted on card stock before drawing the tabs and cutting out the finished garment.

3 After I cut out the mosaic and glued it to handmade paper, I added small scraps of paper matching the mosaic's colors, folded-ribbon flowers, and a strip of vellum to hold Adam in place. I added a punched leaf shape in vellum to the vellum strip. Machine- stitching around the edges added visual interest to the composition.

4 Quotes from the Book of Genesis were typed onto decorative paper imbedded with leaves. I cut out a second piece of handmade paper for the back side and glued a large glassine envelope to the back to hold Adam's wardrobe. Then, I glued the text to the paper and added decorative stitching.

5 I cut a piece of mat board slightly smaller than the front and back. I sandwiched it between the two sheets with acrylic medium, covered it with waxed paper, and allowed it to dry overnight.

" *Do you believe in serendipity? While I was leafing through an old magazine, I came across a reproduction of a 15th-century fresco in the Brancacci Chapel in Florence, Italy. Adam just begged to be outfitted with a fig leaf and more conventional outfits. I remembered somewhere in my stack of saved "stuff" a contemporary Italian magazine page with the word Adam written in mosaic tiles. Some might argue that the creation of this little Garden of Eden was predestined.* **"**

Terry Taylor

Paper Doll Magnets

Simple shapes, bits of embellishment, and sweet faces are all you need to create these charming little dolls. Use your own vintage family photographs to create personalized magnets.

CREATED BY JANE REEVES

MATERIALS

Photographs

Decorative papers

Card stock

Eyelets

Jump rings

Ribbon, lace, buttons, and beads

Magnets

Metal boxes

Acrylic paint

Clip art

Vintage imagery

Acrylic varnish

1 Jane scanned photographs, enlarging or reducing them as needed. She printed out the photographs in black and white.

2 She cut out the heads, arms, and legs separately, then mounted them on card stock. Underneath each head, Jane sketched a simple rectangular shape before cutting it out. Arms and legs were cut out separately.

3 Jane glued decorative paper to each body shape. She punched holes at the shoulders and the bottom of the body and set eyelets in each hole. She repeated the process on each arm and leg.

4 The arms and legs were attached to the body by threading jump rings through the eyelets.

"**My mother loved to tell stories** about growing up in the early years of the 20th century. One of her favorites, repeated often for my delight, described the paper doll apartment house she and her sister created on the back stairs of their house. The characters in this never-ending drama were the Lettie Lane and Betty Bonnet families cut from my grandmother's copies of Ladies' Home Journal.

With this heritage, it's not surprising that I was entranced with paper dolls as soon as I could clutch a pair of blunt-pointed scissors in my chubby fingers. My childhood days were often spent with Gone with the Wind dolls (wish I still had those), dresses of the First Ladies, and the Dionne Quintuplets. There were others as well, too many to list, but I haven't forgotten them. And I haven't forgotten the pleasant time spent with paper dolls.

Now I can make my own, and although they're a bit more ironic and stylized than the old ones, I'm having just as much fun with them."
Jane Reeves

5 Jane glued a magnet on the back of each doll's body, then embellished each doll with ribbon, lace, and beads.

6 To create the box houses for the dolls, Jane sanded the surface of a metal tin. She painted a base coat of acrylic paint on the tin.

7 Jane scanned different vintage images and photographs, sized them as needed, and printed them out. She collaged these elements on the lid of each box, let them dry, and sealed the box with a coat of acrylic varnish. You could embellish the inside of each box if you wish.

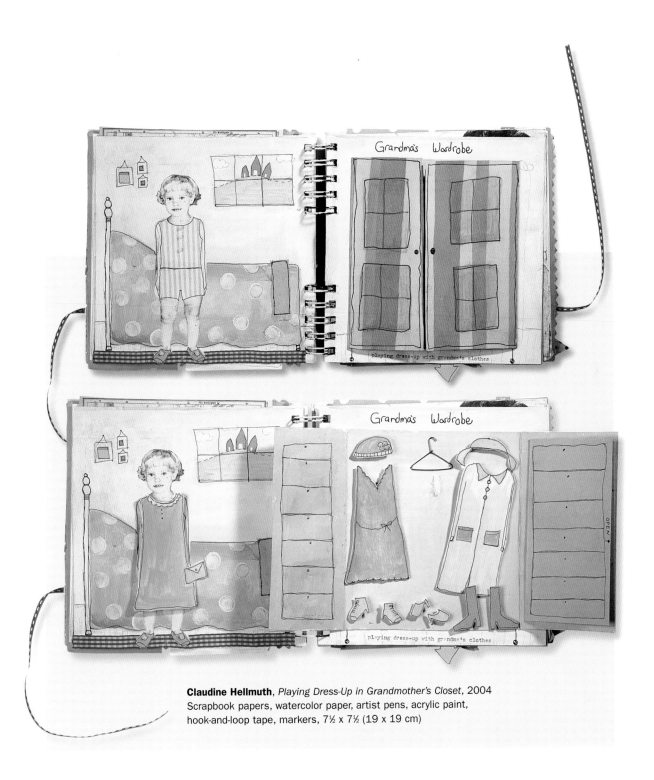

Claudine Hellmuth, *Playing Dress-Up in Grandmother's Closet*, 2004
Scrapbook papers, watercolor paper, artist pens, acrylic paint,
hook-and-loop tape, markers, 7½ x 7½ (19 x 19 cm)

SHRINE DOLL

Carol Owen is well known for her spirit houses and shrines.
Is there a special thought or memory hidden in this mysterious
paper doll's shrine? I don't know, but I suggest that you hide a
secret or a wish in your doll's shrine.

CREATED BY CAROL OWEN

1 Carol drew a broadly defined figure—head, torso, and arms—on card stock and cut it out.

2 She sketched the main form of the shrine body on a single layer of foam-core board. She cut it out, then used the shape as a template to create a second shape. In the center of one shape, Carol cut out a small opening.

3 Carol glued the shrine shapes together with acrylic medium. She used acrylic medium to adhere a layer of rice paper on the shrine shape. After the rice paper dried, she added color with acrylic paint and collaged decorative papers.

4 An assortment of decorative papers was collaged onto the body shape for visual interest.

5 Carol collaged a face onto the body. She then attached the shrine shape to the torso with acrylic medium.

6 Decorative fibers (they remind me of old-fashioned angel hair) were added on top of the collage elements for an otherworldly effect.

Jane Reeves, *Lucky,* 2004
Vintage drawer and candlestick, paper, paint, eyelets, wire, beads, found imagery, 12½ x 6 x 2¾ in. (32 x 15 x 7 cm)

❝❝ ***Paper dolls were the start*** *of my interest in art. When I was very young, I drew my own paper dolls and made my own clothes for them. It was endlessly fascinating to me for a long time.* ❞❞
Carol Owen

TOBY'S HABERDASHERY

Claudine's dog, Toby, doesn't like to play dress up with her, so she made this paper version of him, which she can dress up in cute little hats to her heart's content!

CREATED BY CLAUDINE HELLMUTH

MATERIALS

Photograph of your pet

Watercolor paper

Glue

Colored markers

Acrylic paints

Hook-and-loop
fasteners

House-shaped box
with doors

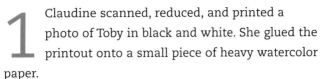

1 Claudine scanned, reduced, and printed a photo of Toby in black and white. She glued the printout onto a small piece of heavy watercolor paper.

2 Subtle touches of color were added to Toby with acrylic paint. Claudine added or enhanced details with markers.

3 Claudine cut out Toby and created an easel stand out of a strip of watercolor paper. She glued the easel stand to the back of the body. A small dot of hook-and-loop fastener was glued to Toby's head.

4 Claudine sketched several hats—a party hat, a crown, and a jaunty bowler—onto watercolor paper. She colored them with paint, adding details with markers. After cutting them out, a small dot of hook-and-loop fastener was glued to the back of each hat.

5 The house was decorated with acrylic paints. Claudine added tiny details with markers and pens. Claudine drew a bone, ball, and water bowl on watercolor paper, colored them, and cut them out. Then she added these elements to the house. She glued small dots of hook-and-loop fastener to the inside of each door, one for each hat.

6 Every house needs a welcome mat, so Claudine created one out of watercolor paper and trimmed it with rickrack.

A Snippet of History

Books and paper dolls are inextricably linked together. Many early paper dolls appeared as regular features in "ladies" magazines of the mid to late 19th century. Understandably, copies of magazines with intact paper doll pages are hard to find. In the early decades of the 20th century, The Delineator featured fiction and nonfiction articles of general interest to women. Early issues featured exceptionally well-illustrated images of the latest fashions for women to copy. In addition, the magazine marketed newly invented paper patterns—the magazine was, after all, published by the Butterick Publishing Co. In addition to educating readers about fashion—prior to the widespread use of photography—paper dolls served to educate readers both young and old about cultures around the world.

In Lettie Lane's Around-the-World Party, drawn by Sheila Young , the lush colors of the drawings, with their careful attention to detail in the costume embroidery, made fine substitutes for photography. A series of these pages featuring children from other countries ran monthly for over two years. *The Ladies Home Journal, September 1, 1910. Courtesy of Magnolia Beauregard's Antiques, Asheville, North Carolina*

> **My earliest paper doll memory** is my mom reading to me the book Jonnesty by Winifred Mantle (Chatto & Windus, 1973). It was a story about a little doll made out of a seedpod. He comes to life, makes friends with a little girl's discarded paper doll, and both run off and live together. I loved the story so much I wanted to create paper dolls of my own so they would come to life and have their own adventures.
> **Claudine Hellmuth**

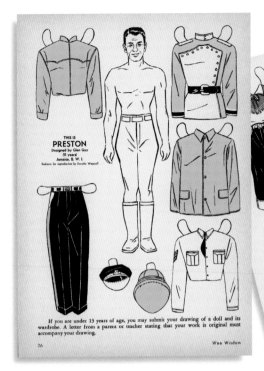

THIS IS
PRESTON
Designed by Glen Guy
(11 years)
Jamaica, B. W. I.
Redrawn for reproduction by Dorothy Wagstaff

If you are under 13 years of age, you may submit your drawing of a doll and its wardrobe. A letter from a parent or teacher stating that your work is original must accompany your drawing.
76   Wee Wisdom

THIS IS
RICKY DEAN
Designed by Esther Brubacher
(11 years)
Redrawn for reproduction by Dorothy Wagstaff

If you are under 13 years of age, you may submit your drawing of a doll and its wardrobe. A letter from a parent or teacher stating that your work is original must accompany your drawing.
26   Wee Wisdom

Pages from *Wee Wisdom*, illustrated by Dorothy Wagstaff in the 1950s.

Movie stars, television personalities, cartoon characters, and even well-known toys have all been published in paper doll book form. Some appeared just once; others appeared over and over again in different editions, sizes, and forms. In the 1930s, Shirley Temple and the Dionne Quintuplets were popular subjects. In the 1950s and 1960s movie stars and dolls based on television series were popular subjects. Even comic books—a book form aimed primarily at boys—offered a small sampling of paper dolls for girls.

The success of Katy Keene (see page 62)—a minor character in the popular Archie series—paved the way for other paper doll comics.

Throughout the 20th century paper dolls were features of mainstream magazines for adults and special interest magazines specifically written for children. In the 1950s *McCall's Magazine* began featuring Betsy McCall (see page 110). Around the same time magazines such as *Wee Wisdom* and *Jack and Jill* featured paper dolls as well. In *Wee Wisdom*, readers under the age of 13 were asked to send in their drawings of dolls and their wardrobes. The original drawings were redrawn by staff artist Dorothy Wagstaff.

In the 20th century, paper dolls were most likely to be published in book form, for the purpose of being cut out and played with. Rather than fretting over the taboos of book mutilation (before altered books became so popular), it has always been perfectly acceptable to cut up paper doll books. It should come as no surprise that—for collectors—uncut books are more expensive than those that have been obviously played with. When I first saw *The Paper Doll Wedding* (page 108) in uncut condition in an online auction it fetched (to my mind) a stratospheric price. Occasionally, paper doll books tell a story in addition to featuring dolls to be played with.

This issue of fun and fashions with America's most "gal-mourous" models featured Millie and her gal pals Chili, Dolly, and Toni. Contributors from around the United States submitted their clothing (and wig!) designs to be redrawn by artist Stan Lee. *The Blonde Bombshell: Millie The Model, Vol. 1 No.106, January 1962, Vista Publications, Inc., New York, New York*

This charming paper doll book tells the story of a wedding—from sending invitations, baking cakes and goodies for the reception, to the final toss of the bouquet. The final page of the book can be made into a wardrobe for storing the dolls and outfits of the wedding party. *The Paper Doll Wedding, Hilda Miloche and Wilma Kane, 1954, Simon & Schuster Inc., New York, New York*

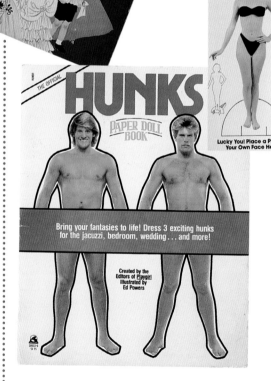

Books for educational play—for both children and adults—were published in the later part of the century. Meant to educate the reader, the topics ranged from coloring books on cultural subjects, such as Kachinas, to tongue-in-cheek looks at modern adult life. Tom Tierney's extensive bibliography of paper doll books includes many historical characters as well as contemporary political figures (see page 114).

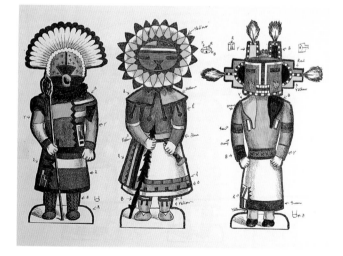

Kachina Dolls *by Eugene & Kay Bischoff, 1952, Eukabi Publishers, Albuquerque, New Mexico*

Your very own photo could be glued onto the face of the female figure to frolic with a young surfer, millionaire, or the macho jock. The hunks had extensive wardrobes; the young lady, basically a wedding dress and nightie. See page 84 for just one of several environments the dolls could play in—the beach, a wedding chapel, and hot tub! *The Official Hunks Paper Doll Book, 1984, Pocket Books, New York, New York.*

Avril Halliday, *Laura's Book,* 2005
Paper book, concertina format, digitally manipulated old photograph, fabric, beads, foils, paint, dried flowers, miniature pencils, stitched, embroidered, 4¼ x 3¼ x 1¼ in. (11 x 8.5 x 3 cm)
PHOTO © ARTIST; COLLECTION MRS. LAURA BEATTIE

Why a Book?

Because there's a traditional link between paper dolls and books, it should come as no surprise that several artists here played with the book format. Each of these artists created a book based on the traditional book format—a cover and bound pages—but interpreted it in innovative ways. A greeting card is constructed somewhat like a simple pamphlet (see page 126). In two examples, the figures' shapes dictated the formats and shapes of the books (see pages 118 and 120). Some artists played with different aspects of altered books—a shaped board book, a repurposed ledger, using alternative materials for book pages. There's even a scrapbook page that uses paper doll ephemera for both inspiration and embellishment. In most of these books and pages there isn't a written narrative; instead, viewers create stories of their own based on their reactions to the imagery. Just what are

those intriguing bird girls buying (page 132)? What tales are those glamour girls telling (page 120)?

I won't tell you how to make a book: We've all made a book at some point in our lives. We couldn't have gone through school without making at least one. We wrote elementary school reports, created special covers for them, then stapled the pages together inside the cover. As we got older, we simply punched holes in the left-hand margin of term papers and threaded the pages onto three-ring binders. The artists who created the books in this chapter used techniques that are simple to replicate: a stitched pamphlet, altered books, or a scrapbook page. If you long to make a book with a Coptic binding, by all means do so. Keep this in mind: It's all about the paper doll; the book form is simply another environment for it.

> **Once while visiting** with my granddaughter Roan, we sat down on the floor in front of her dollhouse with lots of paper, crayons, scissors and glue and began cutting out dishes, placemats, rugs, plates of food and everything else a good dollhouse might need. For storage we made an accordion fold book with pockets to hold everything. Then we had a paper picnic.
> **Claudia Lee**

WHO IS
BETSY MCCALL?

In May 1951, the cover of *McCall's Magazine* pictured a young girl playing with her paper doll. Inside that issue Betsy McCall, the fashion forward five-year-old, came to life amid the pages of a paper wardrobe. In later issues, Betsy acquired an entire paper doll family that included her mother (who remained unnamed); her father, James; cousins Barbara, Sandy and Linda; a friend named Jimmy Weeks; and her most loyal friend, a dachshund named Nosy.

In between regular escapades to the beach, countryside, fashion shows, pet parades, and shopping, Betsy helped promote new McCall's dress patterns as well as designer outfits. Her popularity allowed her to successfully market not only fashion but a way of life as well. Ideal Toy Company recruited Betsy to join their line of three-dimensional dolls and marketed her as a toy with a purpose—to encourage fashion and sewing. The 14-inch (36 cm) plastic incarnation came with a McCall's pattern to make matching child and doll aprons.

By 1953, Rosemary Clooney had paid homage to our heroine in a song called "Betsy, My Paper Doll." That same year, Macy's department store sold a Betsy McCall Halloween costume. Several other non-doll products, including dishes and silverware, also entered the market during the early to mid 1950s.

Betsy McCall waits up for Santa

"I'm going to stay up until Santa comes," announced Betsy on Christmas Eve, "to make sure he doesn't forget a present for Nosy." Mummy hesitated. "All right," she agreed

"Why don't you sit here by the fire?" said Mummy to Betsy and tucked a blanket around her. The flickering fire made Betsy very drowsy. Her head dropped and she was asleep!

Betsy was awakened by Nosy licking her face. Suddenly she remembered—Christmas! "But I was sitting up!" she thought. "What happened?" Then she saw the stockings

One for her and one for Nosy! Santa hadn't forgotten. He'd even brought them upstairs, where she'd find them first thing! So she and Nosy sat up in bed and opened them

This is Betsy McCall

Betsy's nightgown and peignoir were a Christmas present from Aunt Sue

Here are the stockings that Betsy and Nosy hung up on Christmas Eve

Betsy McCall's slip has lace trimming and matches her nylon panties

Betsy opened Aunt Sue's present on Christmas Eve and put it right on!

BETSY McCALL'S LINGERIE BY KAYSER
MAY BE SEEN AT THE STORES LISTED ON PAGE 120

©Copyright 1955 McCall Corporation

Despite competition from her outgoing three-dimensional incarnations, Betsy's presence on paper remained strong for more than 40 years. Even as she grew up and her sense of style and appearance changed, Betsy maintained her charming innocence. Renee Forsyth Ludwig replaced Betsy McCall's first artist, Kay Morrissey, in 1955. Ludwig's much curvier version of Betsy redefined the paper doll's looks for years to come, even after Ginnie Hoffman took over in 1958.

After all the years of modeling the latest fashions, including the eye-catching mod clothes of the 1960s and 1970s, Betsy remained a perfect model of adolescent modesty. Sue Shanahan's contemporary drawings imbue Betsy with a preciousness that captures the hearts of old and new fans alike. Although *McCall's Magazine* had been publishing paper dolls since 1904, they never had a more popular or memorable character than the lovely Betsy McCall.

Betsy McCall
goes to the ballet

"ONE-two-three-four, ONE-two-three-four." It was Betsy's first ballet lesson, and compared to the graceful little children in her class, she felt SO awkward. At the far end of the room, she saw a famous ballerina, Maria Tallchief, practicing before a huge mirror. "I guess SHE was never clumsy," Betsy thought. At the end of the lesson, as the children bowed to the teacher, Betsy was reminded of a field of butterflies. She tried to slide one foot behind the other as they did, but oh, dear, she lost her balance. And the dancer who helped her up was the prima ballerina! Betsy felt like crying, but Miss Tallchief said, "Don't feel ashamed. You'll do it just perfectly, after a few more tries." She reached into her bag, "Here's something that will make you keep working, I know." It was a ticket for the ballet that very afternoon! Betsy sat in the front row and watched her whirl around and around on her pink satin toes. There were cries of BRAVO! and applause, and bouquets and bouquets of beautiful flowers. Miss Tallchief bowed over and over, right in front of Betsy. "Could she be showing me how?" Betsy wondered. Just then, the lovely ballerina tossed her a rose. "Maybe she's telling me I should try it, too." So, guess what! Betsy got up and bowed the nicest bow in return!

This is Betsy McCall

All three of Betsy's dresses are washable. The eyelet-embroidered apron can be removed to show the sweet green cotton dress beneath it

This is the dress Betsy wore to the ballet performance. The detachable pink velvet popover has an eyelet cotton dress under it

Betsy feels like a real ballerina in this fine, imported Swiss-organdy dress. The flower-embroidered apron has border of nylon velvet

COPYRIGHT © 1960 McCALL CORPORATION. BETSY'S DRESSES BY YOLANDE. MAY BE SEEN AT STORES ON PAGE 226. HER PINK TUTU IS BY CAPEZIO.

FOR PAPER DOLLS OF BETSY AND HER COUSIN LINDA, PRINTED IN COLOR ON STURDY CARDBOARD, PLUS 19 NEW COSTUMES TO CUT OUT FOR THEM, SEND 20 CENTS IN COINS (PLEASE DO NOT SEND STAMPS) TO McCALL'S, DEPARTMENT D, P.O. BOX 1290, NEW YORK 17, NEW YORK. IN CANADA: McCALL'S, 462 FRONT STREET WEST, TORONTO 2B, ONTARIO

42

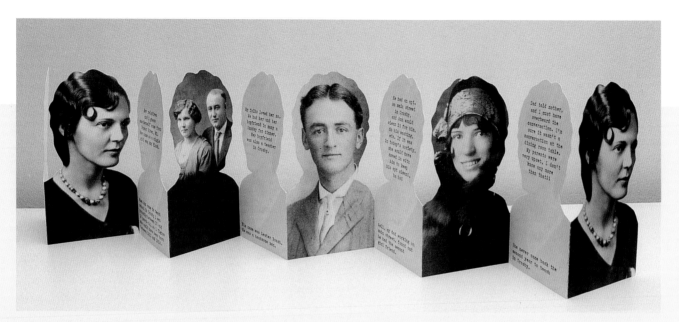

Karen Hanmer, *Ann Black,* 1999
Accordion book, pigment inkjet prints, 6½ x 3½ x 9⁄16 in. closed
(16.5 x 9 x 1.5 cm), 6½ x 19¾ x 3 in. open (16.5 x 50 x 7.5 cm)
PHOTO © ARTIST

Julie A. Fremuth, *It Begs at Me,* 2004
Accordion panel book with jointed figures made from paper, board,
gouache, pencil, colored pencil, house paint, rivets, 8 x 3⅛ x ⅝ in.
(20.5 x 8 x 1.5 cm) closed, 8 x 18 ⅛ in. (20.5 x 46 cm) open
PHOTO © LON HORWEDEL

Pamela Hastings, *Book Doll*, 2005
Papers, copper wire, press-apply letters, colored pencils, paper fasteners, found imagery, rubber stamp, extra-fine point pen, 18 x 8 x ½ in. (45.7 x 20.3 x 1.3 cm)

Karen L. Shelton, *Begin Where You Are*, 2004
Magazine images, white glue, colored pencils, color copies on transparency, rubber stamping, lace, stickers, 12¾ x 8 in. (30 x 20 cm)

TOM TIERNEY'S WORLD
OF PAPER DOLLS

I think I'm a frustrated historian," says Tom Tierney, the illustrator of more than 400 paper doll and fashion coloring books in the past 30 years. Despite his wide-ranging gaze—Tierney's subject matter has included sports figures, storybook characters, and historic costume; world leaders of all eras, such as Pope John Paul II, Queen Elizabeth I, and the American presidents; public figures like Christopher Columbus and Nancy Reagan; and entertainment celebrities from past and present—all his books start the same way: The artist spends considerable time in meticulous library research. He examines the body language and gestures in art of the period, taking note of costume colors. He determines the most appropriate pose, keeping it minimal with arms close to the torso to allow as many clothing options as possible, and selects clothing colors that will keep a flow going through the book. After drawing the figure, he transfers it to illustration board and colors it.

Born in Texas in 1928, Tierney showed promise as an artist from a young age. As a child, Tierney didn't play with paper dolls—they weren't aimed at boys—but he recalls a cousin who bought paper doll books for a dime, and when she asked him to draw extra outfits for them, Tierney agreed to do so. He also remembers seeing paper dolls of the top screen stars of the time, such as Shirley Temple. Hollywood arranged their manufacture, Tierney says. "It was a very shrewd move. It personalized the stars for the kids and captured the young audience."

After college, a two-year stint as a recruiting artist for the U.S. Army, and freelance work illustrating fashions for various department stores in Austin and Houston, Tierney moved to New York in 1954 to pursue a prolific career as a fashion illustrator. In 1975, he contemplated what to give his mother for Christmas. Remembering a collection of paper dolls she had saved from childhood, he hit on the idea of drawing a set of paper dolls modeled on her favorite film stars of the 1930s. His happy mother proudly showed off the trio—Garbo, Gable, and Harlow—to friends and acquaintances. One of these happened to be a literary agent, who convinced Tierney to extend his vision. The following year, Tierney saw the publication of his first book, *Thirty from the '30s*.

Soon another publisher approached him with proposals for more paper doll books. Because the widespread use of photography had caused fashion illustration to become somewhat archaic, Tierney happily launched a successful new phase in his career, one that continues to this day. "It was a fluke!" he exclaims.

When asked if he has a favorite among the many paper dolls he's drawn, Tierney balks. "That's like asking which is your favorite child," he says. But he thinks for a moment, then grants that he might pick Marie Antoinette, the doomed queen of France, portrayed in his book with her dressmaker and confidante, Rose Bertin. Anecdotally, he mentions that Bertin was the first designer to use paper dolls to spread fashion news; previously, real dolls wearing real clothes had passed from hand to hand wearing the latest styles in miniature.

Along with his commercial books, Tierney now self-publishes folios of his dolls. He has also created paper toys such as a Christmas crèche which includes a troupe of musicians and soldiers, and recently created paper dolls of two top film actresses for a style magazine. "I'd love to do a paper doll book on Hollywood hunks," he says, but explains that the idea will have to wait because "men are still considered accessories in the paper doll industry." In the meantime, he's been told that he has the most book rights of any author in the United States. And whether or not his second career was accidental, his paper dolls have been taken seriously; his book featuring Marilyn Monroe even received a review in the *New York Times* literary section.

Tom Tierney

Marie Antoinette

A Paper Doll Book

This is a perfect example of a book used not as a vehicle for story telling, but as an evocation of imagination and mood.

CREATED BY JANICE LOWRY

MATERIALS

Vintage cancelled envelopes

Paper doll dresses

Paper doll

Rubber stamps

Postage stamps

Post cards

Collage imagery

Colored pencils

Book tape

Map

File folder

1 Janice used a variety of different sized envelopes. The windows, stamps, writing, and cancellation marks on the envelopes are decorative in and of themselves. Janice cut them down the sides and flattened them to create the pages.

2 She played with her materials, layering the dresses on top of faces and adding other visually interesting elements such as cancelled stamps.

3 When Janice was satisfied with her pages, she placed them on book tape, and machine-stitched them down the center of the folds.

4 Next, Janice created a cover for the book from a portion of an old file folder. She collaged the heavy stock with a map, rubber stamping, and paper doll imagery.

5 She glued the book tape down the center of the inside cover.

It's not always *that I can make a direct connection between the art I've created and the exact source of inspiration.*

I was reading a Life *magazine dated November 15, 1954, which included an article about the great humanitarian scientist Albert Schweitzer. One of the things he did was to make books out of used envelopes, stitching them down the center with bits of salvaged string. I thought that idea was so fascinating and, as I was laying out my paper dolls, I saw the potential for making some wonderful pages.*

Janice Lowry

ANATOMICAL FLIP BOOK DOLL

At one time, layered anatomical illustrations such as these were the very latest in medical information technology. This 21st Century appropriation of the imagery changes our perceptions of the information.

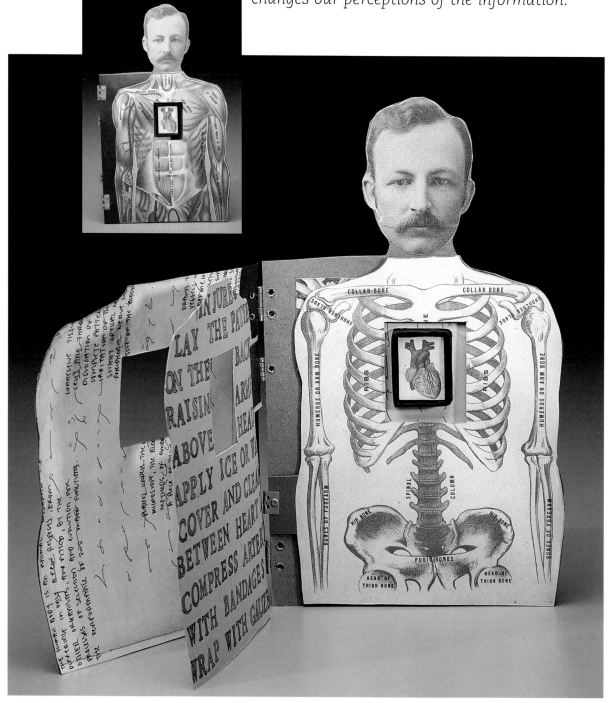

CREATED BY NICOLE MCCONVILLE

MATERIALS

Antique photograph

Anatomical illustrations

Heavy weight card stock

Decorative metal hinges and brads

Decorative card stock

Decorative papers

Tiny papier mâché box

Rubber stamps and inks

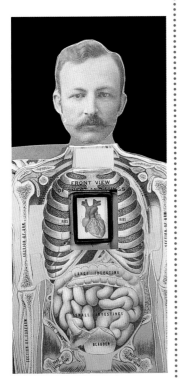

1 Nicole made color copies of vintage anatomical illustrations. The illustrations were bound in the book atop one another—the latest in medical information at the time. She photocopied and enlarged an antique photograph to match proportions of her torso. She cut out the anatomical photocopies, glued them to card stock, and let them dry flat under a heavy book.

2 She glued the head to a large piece of heavy card stock.

3 Nicole cut out the anatomical torso pages, leaving a ½-inch (1 cm) border on the left-hand side of each page.

4 She laid one torso page on top of the heavy cardstock, aligning the torso under the head. She traced around the torso page, then cut out the shape creating the back cover of the book.

5 Hinges were attached to the front and back covers of the body, with additional pages in between.

6 The box was embellished and collaged, then glued to the back cover.

7 Nicole used a sharp craft knife to carefully cut out openings to match the size of the small box on the front cover and interior pages.

8 The reverse side of individual pages were rubber-stamped, painted, collaged, and written upon, much like a journal.

> *As a child* I was drawn to paper dolls for the realm of fantasy and play they represented. The fragility of the paper doll form and the need to handle them with care and attention still appeals to me to this day. I wanted to touch upon that theme of vulnerability with my project. What better subject matter than the human body, created in layers to be touched and explored.
> **Nicole McConville**

GLAMOUR GIRLS BOARD BOOK

Paper doll ephemera are perfect decorative elements for altered books.
Go one step further and create a doll-shaped book, then invite your friends
to collaborate with you.

CREATED BY KIM GRANT, SUSAN MCBRIDE, & TERRY TAYLOR

1 Susan McBride drew the original sketch for the doll, incorporating the curved bottom edges of the board book. I used a small jigsaw to cut out the shape. Then I sent the book to Kim Grant.

2 Kim adhered antique sheet music to her pages with gel medium. After the pages dried, she applied washes of transparent acrylic, which allow the sheet music to peek through the color.

3 Kim applied found imagery and other papers, including the collaged faces, to the pages with gel medium.

4 She drew arms on card stock, cut them out, and added brads to make them moveable before attaching them to the book with brads.

5 Kim added dimensional embellishments: Pearl buttons for a necklace, a length of tape measure for a belt, and paper dots for buttons. Touches of glitter glue applied to the skirts add glamour. Kim entitled her spread "*Oh, How Does My Garden Grow.*"

" *I've always enjoyed paper dolls:* Cutting out the dolls and outfits, then dressing them. But as a child I always seemed to want more than that. I knew there had to be more, but I didn't know what it was I was missing. It was like coloring in a coloring book and having to stay in the lines. I wanted to be set free, to be more creative. I wanted to decorate the edges of the paper with flowing scrolls and doodles of images and words.

Through this paper doll altered book challenge I discovered what I had always been missing: the freedom to create. I needed to add color, texture, and embellishments to make my paper dolls complete. I only wish I had discovered this years ago.
Kim Grant "

6 Susan McBride—aside from being the art director for this book—is a fine illustrator and painter. Her spread, "Opposites Attract," was painted with acrylics.

7 Spanish postcards and ribbon art dolls inspired the cover that I created for the book.

8 I traced around the book to create a dress template on a piece of decorative paper. I collaged images and words from a vintage *Glamour* magazine onto the paper. I gathered the ribbon with basting stitches and machine-stitched the ribbon to the paper.

9 I colored the arms and décolletage on the figure with acrylic paint.

10 Next, I typed text comprised of hair words—bubble cut, bob, chignon, and such—onto colored paper. I cut out the hairdo shape and glued it in place, then collaged a vintage face on top.

11 Finally, I rubber-stamped the title tag, "*Sometimes Glamour is Gaudy*," and added sequins for a touch of tacky sparkle. Of course, no glamour girl is complete without a tasteful strand of pearls.

Spanish Postcards with appliquéd skirts

You can find ribbon art dolls of all shapes and sizes in antique stores and online.
Dol-Lee-Dolls, Wollaston, Massachusetts, and Paterson, New Jersey, 1951

HAPPINESS IS...PAPER DOLLS

There's no reason you can't play with paper dolls, even if you only play with the dresses. You can find a lot of vintage paper doll ephemera online or in antique shops to add colorful and versatile imagery to your paper crafting.

CREATED BY BETH BARUTICH

1 Beth was intrigued when I asked her to create a scrapbook page with paper doll dresses. She didn't have photographs to work with andconsidered purchasing antique photos. Instead, she digitally photographed her niece playing with the dresses that I sent Beth to work with.

2 Beth printed out her photograph in black and white to complement the vintage feel of the dresses. She chose to trim the photograph inan oval shape, rather like an old-fashioned dressing table mirror.

3 Beth used a variety of papers, stacked and layered behind the photo to give the page depth. Rather than gluing the dress flat, she positioned it so that it overlapped the photo.

4 She used paper (meant to look like "old-fashioned primary school paper) for text. Rather than do it herself, Beth asked her older niece to write what she thought about paper dolls on the paper.

Judith Mangiameli, *Asian Paper Dolls*
Wall Assemblage, 2003
Dominos, Japanese papers, Asian coins, chop sticks, porcupine quills, bamboo, found jewelry pieces, 14½ x 11¾ x 3 in. (36.8 x 30 x 7.6 cm)
PHOTO © ARTIST

OH-SO-DRESSY CARDS

Cards are simply pamphlet covers without pages. It would be fun to take this idea further and create entire books of these somewhat unsettling images.

CREATED BY TERRY TAYLOR

MATERIALS

Magazine advertisements

Paper doll dresses

Glue

Card stock

Printed vellum

Vellum envelopes

1 Select magazine images that appeal to you and are close in size to the dresses you have at hand.

2 Cut out dresses and glue them to the images. I like leaving the tabs on the dresses, but you don't have to. After I glued each dress on, I trimmed the image.

3 Fold a piece of card stock in half to create a card, then glue the image to the card. Trim the card to size as needed.

4 I cut an opening in a sheet of vellum slightly smaller than the magazine image. Then I unfolded the card, placed the vellum on top, and machine-stitched the vellum to the card with decorative stitches. On most, but not all of the cards, I glued the vellum cut-out to the inside of the card.

" **Paper doll dresses** *literally littered my office and studio as I wrote this book. While working late one night in the studio, I began leafing through a vintage fashion magazine, spied the Natalie Wood outfits in a pile, and before I knew what hit me, was busily cutting out dresses and fitting them onto advertisements. I especially like the slight disconnect between the figures and the dresses that don't quite fit.* "
Terry Taylor

LA CURANDERA

Like the board book on page 120, the shape of this figure dictated the shape of the book. Coil binding is simple to do yourself, or have it done at your local copy shop.

MATERIALS

Amate paper

Decorative papers

Grommets

Coil binding

Brads

Eyelets

String

Paper ephemera

Acrylic paint

Rubber-stamp images

Waxed linen thread

Charms and milagros

Pop top from soda can

CREATED BY
OPIE & LINDA O'BRIEN

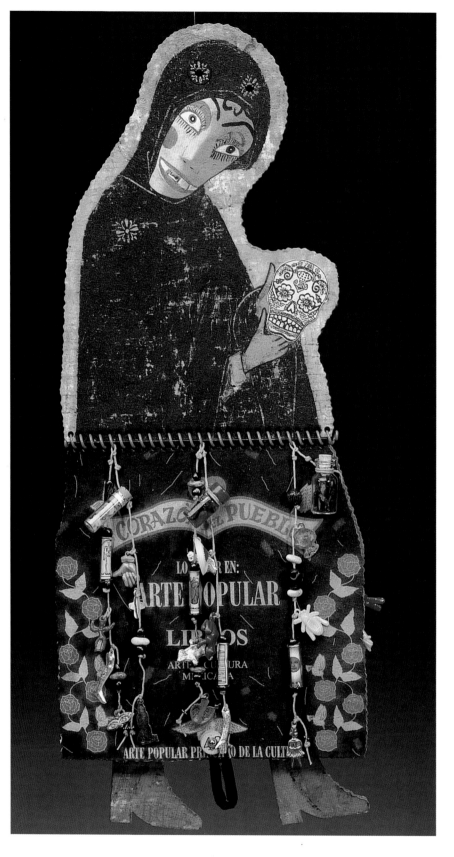

1 Linda and Opie scanned an image from an icon. The scanned image dictated the size and shape of the pages in the book. They added some color to the image with acrylic paint and collaged the face and skull on the figure before mounting it on *amate* paper.

2 They cut out pages using the amate paper and collaged them with a variety of paper ephemera and decorative papers. Color was added to the paper with acrylic paints and rubber-stamp imagery. Additional papers were attached to the pages with brads to create pockets.

*" **A curandero (or curandera for female)** is a traditional folk healer. They are often respected members of their communities, being highly religious and spiritual. Curanderos often used herbs and natural remedies to cure illnesses. Their primary method of healing is rooted in the supernatural, because they believe that many illnesses are caused by evil spirits or curses. The inspiration for this doll came from the paper bag that housed a gallery purchase from a prior trip of ours to Oaxaca, Mexico. We used parts of the actual bag as well as computer scans of the bag. The scans were mounted onto amate paper, a handmade bark paper from Mexico. "*

Opie and Linda O'Brien

3 They cut foot shapes out of thick paper, tinted them with acrylic paint, and attached them to a page with grommets. Eyelets were added to some pages to strengthen holes through which charms would be hung.

4 To assemble the book, Linda and Opie stacked the pages and bound them with a coil binding. Most copy shops will coil-bind books if you don't have the equipment or skills to do so yourself.

5 Linda and Opie threaded charms, milagros, and other dimensional objects onto waxed linen thread. They tied some of the charms onto pages with eyelets and some to the coil binding. A simple pop top from a soda can was stitched to the back to allow the book to hang.

Anna Griffin Inc., *Untitled*, 2004
Vintage photograph, decorative papers, ribbon, reproductions
of vintage figures, 12 x 12 in. (30.5 x 30.5 cm)

Margi Hennen, *Nature Girl*, 2005
Found imagery, brads, 15 x 8 in.
(38 x 20 cm)
PHOTO © DANNY ABRIEL

Anna Griffin Inc., *Untitled*, 2004
Vintage photograph, decorative papers, ribbon, feathers,
reproductions of vintage figures, 12 x 12 in. (30.5 x 30.5 cm)

THE BIRD GIRLS OF HUMBOLDT
"DOLL CUT-OUTS SET №3"

I wish each and every one of you reading this book could hold this gem in your hands. Each page is filled with a wealth of detail. Lucky me, I got to examine it firsthand.

MATERIALS

Vintage ledger

Vintage photographs

Paper doll clothing

Bird images

Poster board

Vintage and contemporary ephemera

Found objects

Mica

Library card pocket

Dressmaker's patterns

Gel medium

Miniature clothespins and fencing

Ribbon

Fabric

Vintage trims

CREATED BY LK LUDWIG

1 LK cut out pictures of bird heads and matched them with dresses she thought suited them. Occasionally, she substituted wings for arms or talons for feet. When she was happy with the effect, she glued the images onto black poster board.

2 On each divider in the ledger, LK adhered one of the ledger entry pages with gel medium. Each ledger page was embellished with different scraps of vintage fabric and other dimensional objects—a plastic teaspoon, scissors, a length of fencing, a dollhouse window, and other items that might have been purchased at the general store.

A few years ago, I found this wooden ledger at a flea market. The ledger had come from Thweatt's Dry Goods in Humboldt, Tennessee. I was initially drawn to its heavy covers, but once I'd opened it, the pages—dated 1939 through 1946—drew me in. The names of the customers, written in longhand at the top of each page, were charming: Mrs. Bitsy Banks, Mrs. Grady Barnett, Mrs. Houston Audon, and others.

I found myself imagining ways to showcase the contents of those pages. I held on to the ledger for quite some time. The carefully listed items—garments and fabrics purchased along with amounts paid—inspired the contents of the book.

These paper dolls—who have rather unusual features—have nested in Humboldt. They have big city dreams but down-to-earth lives. The photographs and the day-to-day accounting of their purchases reflect those lives.

LK Ludwig

3 LK glued a library card pocket to the reverse side of each divider. She glued scraps of ledger entries on the pocket, and filled the pocket with small-scale photographs.

4 Holes were punched in vintage photographs, postcards, and each doll to enable them to be threaded onto the ledger's metal posts.

5 LK used the cover of the journal as another surface for collage. The tiny fabric dress hanging on the clothesline and the girls peering out from behind the fence are charming reminders of an earlier day and time.

DESIGNERS

elinor peace bailey is the author of *Mother Plays with Dolls* (1990) and *The Rag Doll from Plain to Fancy* (1994). She has illustrated books and designed fabric for a variety of manufacturers. elinor is currently experimenting with journaling and altered books, in addition to creating art to wear, which she shows off by wearing herself. She lives in Vancouver, Washington. Visit her website at www.epbdolls.com

Beth Berutich ran out of shoeboxes to store photographs in and entered the scrapbooking frenzy about 10 years ago. Since then, those same shoeboxes overflow with the latest scrapbooking embellishments in her Birmingham, Alabama, home.

Michael de Meng is an assemblage artist living in Missoula, Montana. He has participated in numerous exhibits that promote the awareness of such issues as AIDS, breast cancer, and environmental and social issues. He teaches a variety of mixed media workshops throughout the country. See more of his work at www.michaeldemeng.com

Lisa Glicksman is a mixed media artist living in Oakland, California. She is especially fond of paper arts, rubber-stamping, and painting. Her work appeared in *Altered Art* (Lark Books, 2004).

Mar Goman remembers her mother bringing paper dolls for her to cut out when she was home with childhood illnesses. She calls herself *The Woman Who Can't Stop Making Things*, because she can't. She works in a variety of media including drawing, painting, sculpture and assemblage, collage, fiber arts, and book arts. She's represented by the Francine Seders Gallery in Seattle (www.sedersgallery.com), and shows in several galleries in the Portland area. Mar lives in Portland, Oregon.

Kim Grant works in a variety of mediums and styles but has a fondness for acrylics, watercolors, and collage. She has traveled around the world and taught mixed media workshops in Guatemala, France, Thailand, and Vietnam. Her works can be found in both corporate and private collections. She lives in Chanhassen, Minnesota. Visit her website at www.kimgrantdesigns.com

Pamela Hastings lives in Port Angeles, Washington. Her work has been featured in *Designing the Doll*, *Finishing the Figure*, and *Anatomy of a Doll* (C&T Publishing), *Fiberarts Design Books Four* and *Six* (Lark Books), and *Making Cloth Dolls* (Lark Books). She has self-published three books: *Paper Doll Inspiration Book*, *Designing a Doll and Making Faces*, and *Doll Making as a Transformative Process*. She balances a career in health care with designing, teaching, and making art. Visit her website at www.pamelahastings.com

Claudine Hellmuth is the author of *Collage Discovery Workshop* and *Collage Discovery Workshop: Beyond the Unexpected* (Northlight Books). She lives in Orlando, Florida, and teaches workshops around the world. Visit her website at www.collageartist.com

Dana Irwin is an artist who enjoys an active life with her two dogs and two cats in Asheville, North Carolina. She has taught art at elementary, high school, and college levels. She's an art director at Lark Books and has created projects for many Lark books.

Claudia Lee is a designer, educator, and author. She is the proprietor of Liberty Paper Mill, a working and teaching studio in Liberty, Tennessee. Her designs have been featured in several Lark books. Claudia is also the author of *The Weekend Crafter: Papermaking* (Lark Books, 2001)

Janice Lowry has exhibited her work for more than 30 years. It has appeared in numerous group exhibitions and been featured in *Somerset Studio*, the *Chicago Tribune*, and the *Orange County Register*. She is married with three grown children. She lives near her studio in Santa Ana, California. Her work can be seen at www.JaniceLowry.com

LK Ludwig is a photographer and mixed-media artist living in western Pennsylvania. Her work has been shown in numerous galleries and magazines such as *Somerset Studio*, *Belle Armoire*, *Artitude* and others. Her work has also been featured in *Making Journals by Hand* (Quarry, 2000) and *Altered Books, Collaborative Journals and Other Adventures in Bookmaking* (Rockport Books, 2003). Visit her website at www.gryphonsfeather.typepad.com

Natascha Luther works as a full-time teacher in Dortmund, Germany. Historic costuming is her second passion. When she's not working on mixed-media projects, you'll find her sewing clothing for reenactments. She lives in a large live-in studio with her partner and cat. You can see her clothing, mixed-media work, and rubber-stamp designs at www.taschasbastelkasten.de

Susan McBride is an artist who has worked in the field of graphic design for the last 20 years. She has sketched and painted all of her life. In her workaday life, she's an art director at Lark Books. She's the author and illustrator of *The Don't-Get-Caught Doodle Notebook* (Lark Books, 2005) and *The I'm-so-Bored-Doodle Notebook* (Lark Books, 2006). She lives in Asheville, North Carolina, with her family, two cats, and a dog.

Nicole McConville is an artist with an interest in collage and assemblage, with a particular focus on salvaging found objects. She lives in Asheville, North Carolina, with her mad scientist husband and circus dog in training, in a former bank building they renovated themselves. When she's not tinkering in her studio or burying her nose in a book, Nicole keeps busy attempting to play the accordion. View more of her work at www.sigilation.com

Jane Maxwell is a collage artist whose recent work alters paper doll cut out forms to comment on societal pressure placed on women about weight and body image. Her work has been featured in exhibitions throughout New England and beyond, and also appears in *Collage for the Soul* (Rockport Books, 2003) and in *Altered Books, Collaborative Journals and Other Adventures in Bookmaking* (Rockport Books, 2003.) Jane lives with her husband and three children in Newton, Massachusetts. View more of her work at www.janemaxwell.com

Eric Allen Montgomery is a mixed-media sculptor and glass artist living and working on the west coast of British Columbia, Canada. By day he creates custom corporate recognition gifts and awards. By night, he plays with vintage toys and tools, old photos, and fragments and rusty bits to create his unique memory boxes. He hopes to someday become completely nocturnal.

Jean Tomaso Moore is a mixed-media artist who has created projects for several Lark books, most recently in *Altered Art* (Lark Books, 2004). Jean lives in Asheville, North Carolina, with her funky, guitarist husband, Richard.

Opie and Linda O'Brian are mixed-media artists, authors and teachers, who enjoy pushing the envelope in a myriad of ways, using organic, recycled and found materials. They teach at workshops in the United States, Mexico, and Europe. They are the authors of *Metal Craft Discovery Workshop* (North Light, 2005). Their work has also been featured in *Belle Armoire*, *Art Doll Quarterly*, *Somerset Studio*, *Legacy* and the *Craft Report* as well as in art galleries, museum gift shops. They live in Ohio on Lake Erie with their cat Angelus and his cat Angel. For more information about the artists, visit their website at www.burntofferings.com.

Lina Trudeau Olson is an elementary art educator in Asheville, North Carolina. Her time is balanced between the classroom, the studio, and her young family. She finds this lively mix to be a constant source of inspiration and enthusiasm. Her work was recently published in *Altered Art* (Lark Books, 2004).

Carol Owen is a mixed-media artist who creates Spirit Houses using vintage photos and found objects to tell family stories. She is the author of *Crafting Personal Shrines* (Lark Books, 2004). Carol lives in Pittsboro, North Carolina.

Jane Reeves is primarily known her art quilts that have been included in *Quilt National* and other exhibitions. Her work is found in numerous corporate and private collections in the United States, Saudi Arabia, and Japan. She lives in Black Mountain, North Carolina.

Terry Taylor is the author of *Altered Art* (Lark Books, 2004) and *The New Crochet* (Lark Books, 2005). When he's not working on books or projects for Lark books, he's a mixed-media artist and jeweler. He has studied jewelry and metalwork at John C. Campbell Folk School, Appalachian Center for Crafts, and Haystack Mountain School of Crafts.

Shannon Yokeley thanks her lucky stars that she was born in the computer age; she's truly an egghead. Her interests include Japanese *anime*, collecting oddities, and graphic arts. She's a superhero in the art department at Lark Books—saving files and upholding deadlines. She lives in Asheville, North Carolina.

TEMPLATES

Enlarge or reduce these templates as desired.

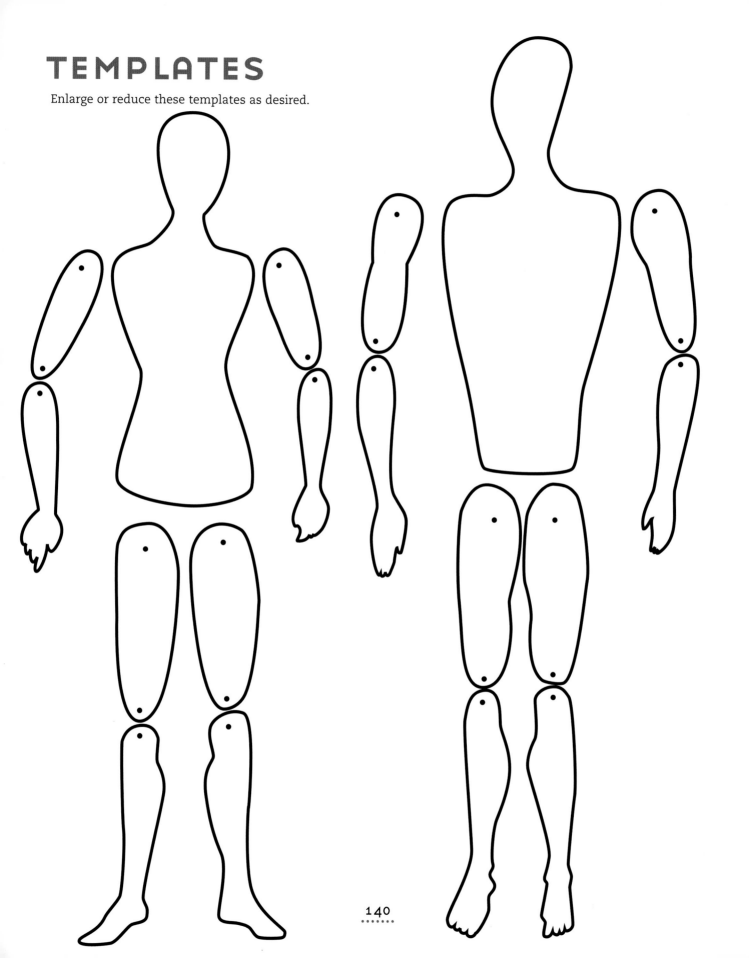

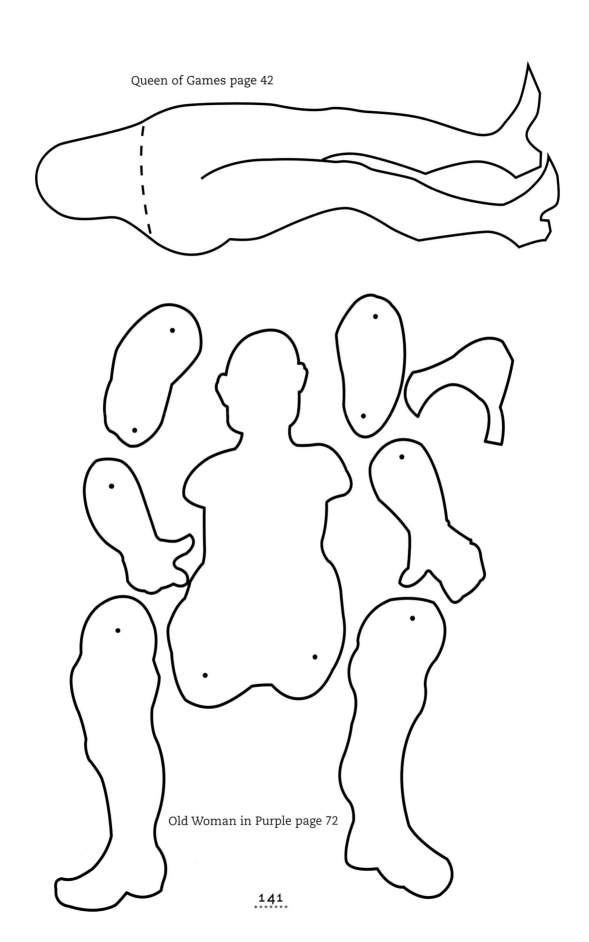

Queen of Games page 42

Old Woman in Purple page 72

Questioning Man page 44

INDEX

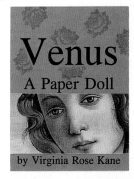

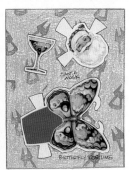

Virginia Rose Kane, *Venus: A Paper Doll,* 1993
Booklet, 5⅛ x 3⅞ inches (13 x 10 cm)
Crayon, rubber stamp, colored pencil, found imagery
PHOTO © ARTIST

DEDICATION

Artful Paper Dolls is dedicated to the memory
of my mother, Faye Taylor. She actively
encouraged and supported my urge to create
from an early age. And no matter what I made,
it was wonderful in her eyes—even when she
didn't understand why in the world
I had made it.

TBT